Gifts of Sobriety

"Barbara S. Cole has a beautiful, at times poetic, way of describing the gifts held within the promises of sobriety. This is a book to read when hope and gratitude have been distant friends."
—Craig Nakken, M.S.W.
Author, *The Addictive Personality*

"Living a life of spiritual principles has its rewards, as described in *Gifts of Sobriety*. Barbara Cole shows readers how to recognize the miracle of recovery as it unfolds in their lives. This book can be a great catalyst for spiritual progress."
—Allen A. Tighe, M.S., C.C.D.C.R.
Hazelden clinical supervisor
and author of *Stop the Chaos*

"*Gifts of Sobriety* is beautifully written, gentle, profoundly human, and utterly positive. Barbara S. Cole illuminates the journey of recovery as full of hope and promises kept. This is a must read for those in early recovery, their families, and those ready for a deeper understanding of the journey they have begun."
—Patricia A. O'Gorman, Ph.D.
Author, *Dancing Backwards in High Heels*
and *Parenting and Addiction*

"Barbara Cole has given the Twelve Promises found in the Big Book the emphasis that they truly deserve. Her book will serve the newcomer as well as the old-timer with a hefty measure of insight and sustenance. I especially appreciated how she interwove the Twelve Promises with the Twelve Steps of Alcoholics Anonymous."
—Karen Casey
Author, *Each Day a New Beginning*

Gifts of Sobriety

WHEN THE PROMISES OF RECOVERY COME TRUE

Barbara S. Cole

HAZELDEN

Hazelden
Center City, Minnesota 55012-0176

1-800-328-0094
1-651-213-4590 (Fax)
www.hazelden.org

Library of Congress Cataloging-in-Publication Data

Cole, Barbara S.
    Gifts of sobriety: when the promises of recovery come true /
    Barbara S. Cole.
        p. cm.
    Includes bibliographical references.
    ISBN: 978-1-56838-354-5
        1. Recovering alcoholics. 2. Alcoholism—Treatment. 3. Alcoholics—
    Rehabilitation—Case studies. 4. Narcotic addicts—Rehabilitation—
    Case studies. 5. Twelve-step programs. I. Title.

    HV5275 .C65 2000
    362.292'8—dc21

                                                            99-086013

Author's note
All the stories in this book are based on actual experiences. The names and
details have been changed to protect the privacy of the people involved. In
some cases, composites have been created. My sincere thanks to all who gave
me permission to use their stories.

Editor's note
The excerpt from the text *Alcoholics Anonymous*, pages 83–84, and the Twelve
Steps are reprinted with permission of Alcoholics Anonymous World Services,
Inc. (AAWS). Permission to reprint this excerpt and the Twelve Steps does not
mean that AAWS has reviewed or approved the contents of this publication, or
that AAWS necessarily agrees with the views expressed herein. AA is a program
of recovery from alcoholism *only*—use of this excerpt and the Twelve Steps in
connection with programs and activities which are patterned after AA, but
which address other problems, or in any other non-AA context, does not imply
otherwise.

15 14 13 12   11 10

Cover design by Lightbourne
Interior design by Nora Koch \Gravel Pit Publications
Typesetting by Nora Koch \Gravel Pit Publications

If we are painstaking about this phase of our development, we will be amazed before we are half way through. We are going to know a new freedom and a new happiness. We will not regret the past nor wish to shut the door on it. We will comprehend the word serenity and we will know peace. No matter how far down the scale we have gone, we will see how our experience can benefit others. That feeling of uselessness and self-pity will disappear. We will lose interest in selfish things and gain interest in our fellows. Self-seeking will slip away. Our whole attitude and outlook upon life will change. Fear of people and of economic insecurity will leave us. We will intuitively know how to handle situations which used to baffle us. We will suddenly realize that God is doing for us what we could not do for ourselves.

Are these extravagant promises? We think not. They are being fulfilled among us—sometimes quickly, sometimes slowly. They will always materialize if we work for them.

—*Alcoholics Anonymous,* third edition,
pages 83–84

CONTENTS

Acknowledgments

This book is dedicated with great love and gratitude to my grandmother Eve Edelstein and my mother, Dee Cache.

I am also grateful to Mrs. Betty Ford and President Gerald Ford for having the courage to change the things they could. I have enjoyed my work at the Betty Ford Center, as my years there have been as healing for me as they have been for my wonderful patients.

Hazelden Information and Educational Services had the good vision to carry this message of hope to those who still suffer from the disease of addiction. I am very grateful for the wisdom, professionalism, and skill of their staff, most especially my editor, Rebecca Post, who is as talented as she is gracious and kind.

Once in a lifetime, special teachers come into our lives, and I have been especially blessed to have had many of the greatest. Of all of these, one has made a very significant impact on me and my clinical work: Dr. Nancy Waite-O'Brien is a master clinician, a gifted public speaker, and a patient, talented teacher. I am grateful for her guidance and friendship. I am most appreciative of Nancy and Terry O'Brien for helping to make this book a reality.

Over the past few years, I have been graced with the presence of many inspiring people who have contributed their friendship, energy, experience, strength, and hope to this project. Of course, I am ever grateful to my Higher Power, In Her Infinite Wisdom, for creating and placing this book in my consciousness at just the right time and place, so that you and those whom you love might be touched by its message. I am grateful to the following people, for their precious friendship and gifts that have multiplied and become far too numerous to mention:

Virginia A.
Dan B.
Julie H.
Patsi H.
Alan M.
Jerry M.
Mike N.
Byron P.
Patty P.
Juliea B.
Julie L.
Dr. Earle M.
Dr. James W. West
Dr. Gail S.
Dr. Gary Nye
Dr. Nancy Waite-O'Brien
1555 Women's Discussion Meeting
Mr. Terry O'Brien
Susan Cruz and her beautiful family
Dennis Hayes
Susan Berkman
Carole Johnson

Introduction: The Promises of Sobriety

Why should anyone undertake the painful journey to be free of alcohol or drug addiction? It is so easy to turn a deaf ear to the impending reality of the consequences that addiction brings, so very easy to put off the inevitable fear and discomfort of withdrawal. It is easy to continue to believe that if only we can find just one more way to prolong drinking and drug use, the mystical, magical *something* will appear and relieve us of our devastating shame and embarrassment that continued use brings. Loss after loss, tragedy after senseless, avoidable tragedy, we or our loved ones afflicted with addictive disease find it easier to forge ahead, trying everything we know to minimize the maddening, debilitating consequences.

Hitting a wall of truth may appear, at the outset, to be something one should avoid at all costs, for it would seem to cause insurmountable pain for us and for others whom we are connected to on a deep, heartfelt level. However, there are good reasons to intervene in the cycle of addiction. Sadly, it doesn't often appear to make great sense to intervene until the consequences of the addiction have mounted to an intolerable point. The primary good reasons to intervene may be those of threats to employment, loss of ability to support our families, loss of an important network of acquaintances.

Then there are the secondary reasons, the reasons we attach to what could be called our *ego needs*. Fear of embarrassment, of letting others down, of admitting that we have behaved less than honorably toward those who have held us in high esteem. Fear of recognizing just how deeply we feel any kind of pain from any source. Guilt from participating in helping the addicted person's problem grow worse (we drank or used with this person and now he or she is hurting from it). The fear of the fall from the pedestal that we have worked so hard to

1

develop and protect is so tremendous that it is nearly untouchable, no matter how much we despise the pedestal and how it isolates us from others whom we care about.

We are, after all, kind and loving on the inside and don't wish to cause anyone, including ourselves, disappointment or harm. So we run from the truth of the growing emergency, whether it is about ourselves or someone we care deeply about. We think that the truth will hurt. We think that it will chase the person away.

The Other Side of the Struggle

Despite this great, symbolic wall of fear and concern, we know that in the fringes of our world, here and there, exist a few who have been able to stop drinking and using drugs. They have managed to make sanity out of insanity somehow, and occasionally have put their new sober lives together in a way that looks attractive to us. And we know in our hearts that we can be like them, if only we could muster the courage or the commitment, if only we could get all of the perfect circumstances lined up "just right". . . if only. . . . In other words, somehow, we know a few people in recovery who have shown us that for all the pain of their journey, they have found a new freedom and a new happiness. It intrigues us that this type of freedom and happiness was not available to them before they dealt with this wall.

The faint intrigue that we may feel as we peer into their lives is really the seed, or beginning point, of health. That intrigue is all that the disease of alcoholism and addiction did not yet destroy. Let us begin with little more than our mild curiosity about those who have gone before us to break through the madness and waste that addiction brings.

Why do those who break free of this mad way of life choose to go through what seems as if it will be an insurmountable wild ride? One recovering woman said, "For as much pain as

I've gone through, am I *ever* going to feel as much pleasure? Is there some cosmic balance in all of this?" Good question! Just what is on the other side of the struggle? *The answer to this question is precisely what this book is about.* Sometimes the only way to know what is possible to achieve is to see it being enjoyed by others.

Often overtaken by this disease ourselves, we are weakened in our faith, health, and ability to even imagine what life will be like if we only persevere in getting and staying sober. Fortunately, the stories in this book celebrate the indisputable fact that people can and do stay sober and, as a result, have marvelous things happen to them. In these pages, you will read the stories of people who have managed to surrender to the disease of alcoholism and addiction in order to free up their energy for pursuits that are life-giving instead of life-taking. They surrender the war to win it. They will share with you how they now regard their full, free, rewarding lives.

Millions Have Gone Ahead

Sometimes it is necessary to know that you or someone you love is not going to be the pioneer, or the first one, to see if such a thing as total abstinence from all mood-altering substances is possible. Fortunately for you and yours, millions of people have gone ahead, freed of the compulsion to drink and use any other mood-altering substance, and have built new lives that are full of the gifts of sobriety.

Here, in these pages, those who have gone before you will share why it makes terrific sense to face their worst fears, risk "rocking the boat," and bravely move into the next phase of their lives: the wondrous phase of life that is entirely free from the negativity and destruction of drugs and alcohol. They are free to love, free to learn new things, free to make changes no matter how painful the process, and free to enjoy the outcome of their transformation from negative to positive, isolated to connected, self-hate to self-love.

This book is made for giving. It is created for those who need to remember the struggle from whence they came. It is made for those who are about to embark upon an amazing journey of transformation. It is made for the merely curious. There is nothing wrong with timidly peeking into a new world way before deciding to set out on the journey toward that world. This journey leads to complete connection without the gauze of numbness that eventually suffocates the victim. Nobody guarantees that this journey will be easy. It took time to create the problem. It will take time to resolve it. It will not be as easy getting out as it was going in, until the healing process is firmly established. And then, once it takes root and begins to flourish, recovery will be the easiest, simplest thing in the world.

This book is also for helping family members understand the worthiness of this journey toward sanity. It is often difficult to stomach one's understanding that addiction drags everybody into the problem, on every scale and level imaginable.

However, touch this problem in a positive way and touch the solution for everybody. Addictive disease has spread throughout our families and our culture, but it is not so stalwart that it cannot be put in permanent remission. The hopeful part of this is that, although alcoholism and addiction is a disease, it is one which can be lived with graciously. Conscious awareness of it, also called the breaking of denial, is as effective to addictive disease as pouring disinfectant over bacteria. It is a relief to know what the possibilities are and that, ultimately, lending one's time, money, emotions, and energy may very well result in something more meaningful than mere temporary relief from consequences. Often even a remote glimpse of what this relief looks and feels like to others is enough to keep a spouse from leaving a committed relationship five minutes before the miracle occurs.

Uncovering the Real Self

Sometimes seeing reality results in just the opposite outcome, as the person puzzled about how to improve the quality of his or her life finally achieves some real-world clarity and understanding. Sobriety often brings long pent-up truth to a given situation. Even if painful, rarely is facing the truth not a relief in the long run.

When we are actively addicted to a substance, we cover up something precious that only those closest to us can see. This precious something is our real self. Despite our attempts to cover up our true, vulnerable selves to hide the mess of our addicted lives, still the original spirit inside peeks through here and there. A beautiful soul rarely refuses to be covered up without a decent fight. When the soul fights, those who love us see it. And those who love us see this truth about ourselves that we may not be able to see any longer. They often work (too) hard to convince us of a goodness in ourselves that we can only disbelieve the more they try. To see it, to believe them, is to begin cutting through the trickery of the disease.

Because it is the nature of this disease to catch others in the web of illness, often the people closest to us, those who still believe in us and see our goodness, grow weary of being involved in our sickness and chaos. The afflicted person is then steeped in guilt and shame as consequences from drinking and using drugs mount and take an ever greater toll. This person feels increasingly ugly, pitiful, and hopeless until there is simply a desire to give up. All too often, this means giving up on life itself. Utter hopelessness and despair are one of the final symptoms of the disease. To break through the hopelessness, a loving vision can be helpful. In the end, it is love that holds on to hope and love that grasps for the promise of something better. Perhaps this book, based upon such promises, given in the spirit of goodwill and kindness, will provide just that special vision.

Here, then, is hope for the alcoholic or addict who still suffers from this disease, as well as for their loved ones. Even if you are not currently drinking or using, you may still suffer from the secondary effects of doing so. Take heart. Embedded in the stories of those who have lived through the early years of sobriety are messages of amazement, relief, satisfaction, serenity, sanity, healing, joy, meaning, purpose, and peace. It is hoped that these messages will inspire you to embark upon your own journey. If you have already started the journey, may you be heartened to know what is ahead. How will you know the trail marks of health as you come upon them unless someone tells you what the marks look like?

The Promises

There are promises made to those who wonder just why they ought to give up their terrible relationship with alcohol and drugs. These promises are the trail marks by which one can know one's progress in the journey toward health. In the program of Alcoholics Anonymous, there is a book called *Alcoholics Anonymous,* often referred to as "The Big Book." This book contains a quite remarkable passage, referred to as "The Promises."[1] This passage imparts the following information regarding the trail marks mentioned above:

1. We are going to know a new freedom and a new happiness.
2. We will not regret the past nor wish to shut the door on it.
3. We will comprehend the word serenity and we will know peace.
4. No matter how far down the scale we have gone, we will see how our experience can benefit others.
5. That feeling of uselessness and self-pity will disappear.

---

1. *Alcoholics Anonymous,* 3d ed. (New York: Alcoholics Anonymous World Services, Inc., 1976), 83–84. Reprinted with permission. (See editor's note on copyright page.)

6. We will lose interest in selfish things and gain interest in our fellows.

7. Self-seeking will slip away.

8. Our whole attitude and outlook upon life will change.

9. Fear of people and of economic insecurity will leave us.

10. We will intuitively know how to handle situations which used to baffle us.

11. We will suddenly realize that God is doing for us what we could not do for ourselves.

12. [These promises] will always materialize if we work for them.

Many have believed in the reality of these Promises and some have achieved long-term sobriety just on the faith that these Promises existed! Just a select few of the many millions who have achieved a life of living the Promises of Sobriety on a daily basis have shared their experience, strength, and hope here. What an incredible gift that their sharing can be if any of the words you read in this book inspire you to discover your own gifts of sobriety.

CHAPTER ONE
We Are Going to Know a New Freedom and a New Happiness

Today I take the first step toward my new life by allowing myself to believe that I have a right to be free and happy no matter what.

Freedom is a powerful concept. Since ancient times, we as human beings have been willing to risk death for a chance at freedom of one type or another. Freedom from hunger, isolation, and danger are some of the fundamental freedoms we strive for in the present. These represent basic needs that must be met in one way or another. Certainly there are other basic needs besides freedom, but freedom is right up there with such primary needs as affection and food. As humans, we must first meet these needs before we can focus on anything that uses our more socialized, learned talents, skills, and abilities.

Think of a starving sculptor. What is her first priority? How can she be free to use her refined artistic skills when most of her attention is attuned to satisfying her need for food? The physical needs are easy to talk about because they are universal and the most obvious. For example, we all need food, sleep, and shelter. But we also have needs that are not as obvious. We need affection, validation, social connection, and a sense of purpose in life. These are not all of our needs but a good beginning list. As people who are addicted to substances, or as those who love such people, we must place our precious need for freedom at the top of this list.

The need for freedom is as fundamental as the need for food, shelter, validation, and social connection. Let's use the above example of the sculptor, only now substituting her hunger for

9

freedom for her hunger for food. If she is increasingly focused on her need to free herself of some type of bondage, how can she express her more refined talents? Her primary attention will be on the fundamental task of gaining freedom first and foremost. Once this has been achieved, then and only then will she be able to clearly focus on goals that are less urgent.

Freedom Is a Birthright

It is important to recognize that freedom is not negotiable. It is not second to other needs. In fact, freedom is a fundamental, basic human need, and to acknowledge this from the beginning of our journey of understanding the first Promise of Sobriety—"We will know a new freedom and a new happiness"—is to understand the relationship that freedom has to the basic idea of sobriety itself.

Someone once said that the creators of these Promises must have been listening to and speaking the very words of God. In other words, these Promises wisely recognize who we are and what we need to know to be armed for the battle of wresting ourselves back from the oppression of disease. As people who recognize that we have a problem with alcohol or drugs, or as those who care about us, we absolutely must know that working toward freedom is a healthy, realistic, and obtainable goal. Freedom is a primary goody, as it were, and we may begin to feel the glee and expansiveness of it even in the first moments of our decision to be free of our addiction, long before the alcohol or drug has left our bodies.

Very few among us are made to be pioneers. Most of us have to know what we are getting ourselves into well before we are willing to jump in. In fact, we are all about fear. Fear is controlling, all-encompassing, suffocating, predictive, and death oriented. Fear is just what addictive disease is all about. Freedom from a fear-based life is well worth checking into. But being one of the first to see if this is a possibility is way too frightening for a fear-based person such as an addict. Therefore, we need a great deal of assurance and reassurance to reach beyond our built-in fear for the specter of freedom from it. We want to be positive that such a freedom is possible before we rock the boat, let others know that we have a problem by seeking help for it, or risk upsetting someone by acknowledging that we have noticed that he or she has a drug or alcohol problem. Fortunately, the gift of assurance can be found in this very first Promise of Sobriety.

This Promise, "We will know a new freedom and a new happiness," does not say that we *may* feel a new freedom; it makes a very firm statement that we *will* know, as a result of sobriety, a new freedom. In fact, if you go back a few pages, you will find a numeric listing of all of the Promises (pages 6–7). Please review them, noting their tone above all else. Notice that all of the Promises are firm, nonnegotiable statements. As you read them, they sound absolute and strong. Although they may seem far-fetched at the beginning of the journey toward sobriety, these Promises are as solid and as believable as the hand you are using to hold this book.

From the moment you decide to leave addiction behind, by breaking the denial surrounding the addiction, this First Promise begins to come true. Just because we are not yet able to notice that it is coming true does not mean it isn't. Soon we will be able to effect a change in our perception of things. We will become more sensitized to our surroundings. Our growing sobriety will allow us to see the positive progress that we have made in enjoying our new freedom.

If we care about someone who is addicted, then the same holds true but in a slightly different way. We may be so used to the routine of dishonesty, manipulation, caretaking, and disappointment that when it subsides or disappears altogether, we have a difficult time noticing the positive change. Instead, we may try to sabotage the new sobriety and positive progress, to bring things back to the way they once were. After all, if we are being honest with ourselves, we, too, are participants in a fear-based addictive system, even though we may never ingest mood-altering substances ourselves. And being a participant in such a negative system, we are just as fear-based as the addict or alcoholic. Change frightens us. The First Promise of Sobriety applies to us, too, because, if we work for it, we will know a new freedom and a new happiness based on new habits, expectations, and behaviors. And when these behaviors begin to change, we will welcome them and allow ourselves to note the positive effect they are having on our lives, even if we are uncomfortable while this transition is occurring.

Freedom and Powerlessness

Now why is the subject of freedom packed into the First Promise and not, say, the Third Promise? One recovering gentleman stated that perhaps "the Twelve Steps of Alcoholics Anonymous were meant to be answered by the Twelve Promises." This being the case, the First Step of Alcoholics Anonymous, "We admitted we were powerless over alcohol and that our lives had become unmanageable" is answered by "We will know a new freedom and a new happiness."

The First Step talks about powerlessness. The First Promise talks about freedom, which is also known as empowerment. One answers the other. Take a Step, begin to realize the blessings of a Promise. Take another, realize another.

Earlier in this chapter we noted that freedom is a fundamental human need. So, of course, the first thing that the disease of addiction takes from us is this most precious of our birthrights: freedom. It makes sense, then, to place this Promise first on the list of all Twelve Promises. Logically enough, the first thing one gets back after breaking through the denial about addiction is freedom. The first thing taken by the disease is the first thing given back once we choose to surrender our war with it. How beautiful and how simple this is. It is not a coincidence that beauty and simplicity are the antithesis of the disease of addiction.

One recovering woman said, "If I knew how simple it was to live a good life without alcohol, I might have felt ready to get and stay sober sooner. I used the idea of this process being ridiculously complex as one of the reasons to continue procrastinating and continue using."

Take a moment to write down the loss of freedoms that you have experienced as a direct result of drugs or alcohol in your life. For example, have you or someone close to you lost driving privileges? What about the trust of your co-workers and family? Are you no longer allowed to baby-sit your grandchildren? Do you have to worry and lose precious time figuring out where you are getting your next supply of alcohol or drugs? Do you lose serenity because you are trying to second-guess what your addicted friend, relative, or significant other is going to think or do next? Are you no longer in touch with people you used to care about? It may be difficult to be blatantly honest with yourself. If you are even willing to consider making such a list, then you are nearly ready to experience the gift of the First Promise. If you are not, what *are* you willing to do to regain your freedom from limitations, health problems, and lies? On the back of the same sheet of paper, first think about and then write down what you imagined freedom from each of these losses will be like.

Does it help to see what this loss and gain of freedom looks like on paper? The Promises are amazing because they are so personal. Each of us understands freedom in a different way. But the Promises of Sobriety cannot help but begin to come true with even the smallest willingness to do the work. Because with the first healing of the first brain cell, with the first keeping of a conviction or a vow made to another, with the first expansion of the attention span or recovery of one's short-term memory, comes a new freedom. Voilà. This Promise is fulfilled before we are halfway through. But wait, there's more!

Who's in Charge?

This Promise tells us that, without a doubt, freedom from the many different types of slavery imposed upon addicts, alcoholics, and those connected to them is not merely a possibility, but an inevitable outcome. This guarantee is built into the reality of each and every action we take to make it so.

Being addicted to any mood-altering substance is to be enslaved. Paradoxically, addicts and alcoholics, people who have become enslaved by chemicals, typically have a strong difficulty in dealing with authority figures! This might be amusing if it weren't so tragic. We figure somewhere along the way that we will live our lives the way that we want to, that nobody will tell us what to do. And the way that we want to live, we tell ourselves, includes using chemicals to enhance or change our perception, no matter what negative results this behavior causes. We act as our own authority, or so we think. Doing it "our way," we figure that we are free. And here begins the madness of addiction.

The chemical sooner or later becomes the authority. We have to answer to it. We act as it dictates to support it; we feed it as it dictates to support it; and instead of freedom, it gives us slavery as it gains power over us and those we care about, with every tick of the clock. We are as un-free as it gets. But in order to avoid painful withdrawal symptoms and all of the attendant social problems that total abstinence brings us in the short term, we practice the ridiculous, finding interesting new ways to justify insane thinking in our lives.

The disease of addiction would love for us to continue this type of thinking. How quickly we lose our freedom and belong to

It. It would not be strange or wrong to personify the disease as an It. It behaves like a calculating dictator or a master event planner.

Just like any dictator, first It overcomes our sense of history of ourselves. Next, It disengages us from our strong connections with others. Third, It pulls us away from any sense of being connected to a higher order or spiritual power greater than ourselves. It makes us believe that we stand alone, that we are in charge of our complete destiny, all by ourselves. Then, when we are dying of shame and embarrassment for the mess that we, acting as God, have made of our lives, there It is to salve the wound. It gives near-perfect relief from emotional pain. But take heed of the words *near perfect.* Where It fails are in two key areas: First, It gives near-perfect relief from emotional pain but takes, as Its price, our most precious strength—our emotions themselves. Second, over time It ceases to give us anything and begins to take our health. Most of us begin using and drinking to control the way that we see things, how we do things, and how we feel. Eventually most of us find that we have lost this ability through drugs and alcohol and are trapped by the substances themselves in a cycle of avoiding the emotional and physical pain and related consequences that It, Itself, brings to us.

What a convenient, deathly perfect cycle we are caught up in. Trapped. It is there to quiet the sorry, sick reality that we really aren't the master of our own affairs. Is anything more intelligent than It? If you already know the answer to that particular question, you likely are appreciating many gifts that are spoken of in these Promises.

Cunning, Baffling, and Powerful

Since the disease uses our best traits and talents, and even uses our intelligence for Its own longevity and survival, it is often said that It, known as the disease of addiction, is "cunning, baffling, and powerful." It is an enslaving enemy that appears from the inside as a friend. It is so well camouflaged that even when our dearest and closest family members and friends catch It and tell us about It, we think they are nuts, misinformed, vindictive, jealous, mean-spirited, or have some other agenda.

By the time someone else tells us that we have a problem, the problem is so far out of hand that we probably won't be able to see it. The disease of addiction, when It is in full bloom, conceals Itself better and better by poisoning our own perception of ourselves. Nothing is further away from freedom than that.

The kind of freedom we are rewarded with in a life of abstinence from drugs and alcohol is, on a different, more immediate scale, a version of the same freedom that so many have died for. Many who have struggled with the terrible bondage of addiction have lost the battle and died. The horror of this disease does not stop at the death of the addict or alcoholic, however. Unfortunately, It slowly works Its dark magic into a family, a community, and a whole society and takes directly and indirectly related hostages alike.

One becomes a hostage to the disease of addiction when the disease skews our perception so that we are not thinking of acting in a healthful, supportive way. We only *think* that we are. However, the promise of enjoying freedom and happiness on a daily basis has come true for those who know how to "see It" through their newly opened eyes. Healing from this disease, among other things, requires a dramatic shift in perception. The old way of seeing things only supports addiction and so must be cast off as useless baggage as we venture into our new lives.

The paradox of addiction is that the more we struggle with our addiction and addictive behavior, the more attached we become to the disease and are conquered by It. Some spiders use this method of catching their prey and it is most effective. Quicksand is supposed to work this way too. Our first instinct is to fight against the disease with all our might. We are told over and over again, when it comes to quicksand and tarpits, spider webs and riptides . . . all natural things that are more powerful than we are: Don't fight it! Accept it.

To gain freedom from the insanity of this disease, we must treat It the same way that a body surfer would treat a riptide: Surrender to the power of this force and accept Its power as absolute. This gives you the objectivity to understand It, to be separate from It, to preserve your resources while under Its influence, and then to slowly but surely separate yourself from Its deathly pull.

Acceptance and surrender signal the beginning of attainment of freedom and happiness. If you are using this book as part of a discussion group, note the arguments and difficulties that newcomers have so that you can feel grateful for how far you have come in your understanding and healing process.

Please remember to have patience and empathy for people who struggle with this concept of acceptance and surrender. Many of us in the Western world were raised to believe that just the opposite concept is true. These beliefs include (1) that we must have self-control, (2) that we must pull ourselves up by our own bootstraps by sheer force of will, (3) that we are weak if we have no willpower, and (4) that human mightiness in spirit or action will overcome anything. In the case of most unconquerable forces, such as this disease, it takes a great deal of blind faith, support, positive example, practice, and courage to move away from such ingrained, basic belief systems that oppose the idea of acceptance and surrender. Some of us already know this and are alive and thriving as living proof that the paradox of acceptance and surrender works. Most who suffer from this disease in some way, however, do not know this. Our patience and empathy while others work their way toward this understanding are imperative.

Defining Freedom

Let's move on to how this concept of freedom and happiness affects people in the everyday sense. Freedom is defined by the person experiencing it. For one recovering woman, this is experienced as having a means to deal with the oppression of negative feelings:

"One day, while I was driving down the road, a song came on the radio. I felt this horrible pain for what the song was reminding me of. I felt awful. Burdened. Just then, I remembered what Martha, my sponsor, told me to do whenever this happened to me, and this happened to me quite often, unfortunately. I rolled down the window of my car, visualized pulling the burden of this pain from the inside of me to the outside of me, put it into my hand, and threw it out the window. So whenever I get that pain, the kind that puts a brick in my chest, I tell myself, 'Yes, I did that. Yes, it was awful. Yes, I embarrassed myself. And yes, I don't need to do that anymore. I don't need this particular feeling.'

"I physically roll down the window and throw it out. What I have learned is that holding on to negative feelings sabotages my sobriety. I never know when I'll feel bad or how strongly I'll want to get rid of that feeling. But for today I choose to treat the bad feeling with a good behavior. And for today, I don't have to drink over it. The freedom that I get by having healthier reactions to my feelings of guilt and sadness is worth everything I have and then some. In fact, let me say that everything I have is because of this freedom. I truly cherish every moment of my sober life because of it."

For others, the growth process that naturally occurs with sobriety brings freedom from a need to appear perfect. The need to appear perfect is often a cover-up for the disease that is growing in Its hunger to usurp, in privacy, the life of the person hosting It. A great sense of freedom comes from removing feelings of shame and guilt which are feared as character flaws.

When perfectionism is used to hide shame and guilt, the addict/alcoholic feels like a "fake." Here is another woman's story about this phenomenon:

"That first year was frightening. It took me two years before I did not feel fragile any longer. Two years before I did not have to put on my 'beautiful' facade because I was afraid that somebody would figure out that I was an alcoholic. When I think of it, the only word that comes to mind is *fragile*. During that first year I was as fragile as spun glass. I was afraid of going back to where I had been when I was drinking. And I had wanted to die back then. Afraid and fragile and bound with a ball and chain to a taskmaster called perfection. False perfection. My sobriety has bought me freedom. Freedom from fear, freedom from the burden of false perfectionism, and freedom from fragility. I will tell you this with certainty: I am not a fragile person! Not anymore. That means that I can handle the times when I look in the mirror and I am not so very beautiful. My idea of what beauty is has changed as a result. My idea is that me being my real self is me in the act of being beautiful."

For others, happiness and freedom are experienced on a less physical, somewhat more philosophical or spiritual level. Often this can feel as though the world has opened up wide and is available to provide riches in the depth of experience. Sometimes happiness is discovered in insights that are not possible when one's brain is focused on the cycle of addiction. Freedom from rigid thinking, freedom from dogma, freedom from constraints that before, while drinking and using drugs, might have felt like a mandatory life experience—liberation from all of this brings tremendous relief and happiness.

During a period of active addictive behavior, the perception of time shifts to either the past or the future. This is because the disease does not thrive in the present. The past is where trauma and injury to the spirit reside. For the addiction to preserve Itself, It requires Its victim to perceive that what is happening now really is the same as what had happened in the past. In this way, old pain and resentments are felt in the present. The feelings of hurt, anger, sadness, guilt, and shame feel overwhelming. To treat these feelings, the alcoholic/addict self-medicates with a substance that numbs or displaces the feeling. It is not long before the substance itself creates a world where past equals present, thus creating more opportunities for the disease to thrive and grow.

Living in the future works in much the same way. When the perception of time shifts to the future, we become highly aware of where we are not, what we are not, and how much further we have to go until we get to a point of defeat. Living in the future creates an instant feeling of inadequacy and anxiety for the alcoholic/addict.

Our nonaddicted loved ones handle their pain similarly. As long as the reality of our behavior, consequences, and declining health can be put in the past or future, our friends, significant others, and family members can survive one more day without having to deal head-on with the disease. And so the disease lives on in all of us.

Addiction preserves Itself by causing Its victim to maintain a future-based viewpoint, mixing insecurity, doubt, and anxiety as Its elixir to guarantee that the alcoholic or addict will seek further solace from these feelings through a drink or a drug.

One of the many gifts that sobriety brings is a new way to experience, redefine, and use one's time. One very wise fellow in recovery described this gift of freedom in terms of understanding time:

"There are two different kinds of time that I have become aware of since really enjoying the fruits of my sobriety. The first kind of time is the physical, organic kind of time. For example, the time it takes you to understand what I'm telling you now. That is called physical time. But people who live the promise of sobriety understand a new freedom because they gain a second type of time. Emotional time. Emotional time is a horse of a different color from physical time. With emotional time, there is no past and there is no future. Whatever happens occurs within any given moment and then it is done. Always."

A Connection with Others

Alcoholics Anonymous suggests this concept of time when it speaks of the twenty-four-hour program, or "One day at a time." But "one day" is too long! Actually, I follow a one-second program: The second-by-second experience of me speaking and you listening or vice versa. The moment we are sharing together. As long as I am free to fully enjoy it with all of my senses available to me, and as long as I am free to let it go and fully enjoy the next second, I am no longer a slave to time. I am free from the burden of controlling behavior, from gluing myself to the past or the future. I move freely from one moment to the next. Nothing is freer or easier than I am at any given sober moment. I know a new freedom and a new happiness because I do not struggle, now that I have left my controlling behavior in many moments past.

The sense of freedom that becomes available to the person in recovery opens up an entirely new world. To live in the present is to face fear and doubt, give up the idea of control and safety, and simply experience each moment as it arrives and leaves, letting it come and go freely without grasping or clinging to it. Some moments bring tenderness, some bring beauty. Some moments bring connection with others, which is, of all of the tools one must use to stay clean and sober, the most important. A strong, heartfelt connection with another human being is not only healing; it also breaks the proverbial back of this disease.

So what about a new freedom and a new happiness? Here's what: We are spending time together, sharing. You listening, me talking, or vice versa. In that moment when we are experiencing one another, with all of our senses available to both of us, what else is there but pure happiness?

Freedom from Dishonesty

Another freedom that many in recovery appreciate is the freedom from dishonesty. Freedom from having to scheme, manipulate, and build a wall of lies between themselves and others. These lies protect the disease from being discovered and intervened upon by siblings, spouses, employers, and friends. It seems that the ones who are the closest and most influential often receive most of our lies.

The shame and guilt we experience for digging ourselves deeper into a grave of dishonesty often contributes to the feeling of hopelessness that accompanies the later stages of addiction. The lies may begin on a small scale and grow and progress quickly into areas that many in recovery still find personally shocking when they think about how far the lying behavior went. Recovery requires honesty. Honesty is an important blessing and a freedom supported by sobriety.

There is tremendous freedom in honesty. Imagine never needing to remember the details of the lies that cover up or minimize our addictions. Imagine waking up feeling psychically "clean" every morning and falling into a blissful, babylike sleep at night, light as a feather because nothing untruthful needs to be carried over to the next day to compound into more lies.

Imagine always speaking your mind without the worry of someone getting too close and discovering the secret of your addiction, which protects Itself from view at the cost of your health and well-being.

Imagine the freedom of a downy dandelion seed in the wind, moving easily, without any struggle, slipping freely over vast stretches of land. You can certainly cover a lot of ground when not heavily burdened by a pack stuffed with lies. Our new freedom is not unlike the dandelion seed in the wind.

Often, one begins to feel this lightness the very moment that denial around having the disease of addiction is broken through. But this light feeling is nothing like the ease and comfort of lightness that is on its way. The most beautiful part of being free from addiction is the excitement of living in the present moment while also feeling excited about what is coming in the next moment. Before, the fear of having our lies and exaggerations found out overshadowed any excitement. Paranoia creates a dark film over everyday joy. How wonderful not to have to stop new things from happening in order to prevent unwanted surprises. How reassuring to experience safety only when it is real and reliable and not when it is falsely constructed into a jail built of lies.

With this freedom that sobriety brings, we can let down our guard. We have more life energy than ever before, because no part of our spirit is being used to protect the self from being found out. There is no longer anything that is threatening to us to be found out. We no longer have to run or hide. We are free to stand our ground.

New Awareness

Another freedom and happiness enjoyed by those in recovery is the ability to experience the world through awakened senses. Touch, smell, hearing, taste, and sight may all have been affected in some way by the disease. The return of precious sensitivity to beauty brings a well-deserved joy to the person who chooses recovery. Here, a recovering woman shares her delight with her gift of sight:

"Since I've been sober, I've received a gift of the enhancement of one of my senses. Ironically, because of trouble that I have had with my eyes, it is an enhancement of enjoyment from my sense of sight. I've enjoyed this gift more than any of the other gifts given to me by my sobriety. I have seen so many things in sobriety that I would never have seen before. When I see them for the first time, I get a euphoric rush, a thrill. The first time I drove on a California highway, I saw not one, but four layers of interstate. They don't have four layers of interstate in the part of the country that I come from. I was grinning, smiling, and laughing. I was so excited at seeing this.

"I was also very excited when I saw my first roadrunner. I thought roadrunners were only in cartoons! I have ridden in a subway, flown in an airplane, viewed not one but two oceans, been to San Francisco, ridden on a trolley car, and hailed taxis. The things that have been most rewarding for me are the things that I have been able to see. It is amazing that, for someone who cannot see too well, with sobriety my sight has broadened and deepened and, along with it, a deep abiding sense of appreciation for this gift."

Some of the most delightful gifts of sobriety are those that are unexpected. For some, the very idea of quality of life is a brand new idea. It's so new, in fact, that it did not even have a definition and was not even a concept before a person gained some clean and sober time. Having quality in your life is very much like enjoying stereo sound rather than a single speaker playing a favorite tune.

Addiction imposes a flatness of experience, a single dimensionality to our thought process, and a tunnel vision of purpose to support Itself. Recovery, on the other hand, brings depth to almost every experience, widens our potential range of feeling, and introduces the idea of gray area and choice to our thought process. These gifts enrich our moment-to-moment living and touch everything and everyone who encounters us in a positive way.

It is not fair to have a life without quality. Quality in one's life is something that is a birthright, and not at all optional. An understanding that one can have quality while living a clean and sober life is a special gift that one woman in recovery highly recommends:

"There is a reason to stay sober. There is a big difference between 'can' stay sober and 'reason' to stay sober. I believe anybody 'can' get sober and stay sober, but I like the portion of the Big Book when it talks about the Fourth and Fifth Step and about how there is quality to our life. That recovery is not just about 'putting the plug in the jug.' It is about having quality in a life. If I can make one experience mandatory for newcomers to a clean and sober life, it would be for them to understand that there can be quality to their lives. That is the thing that kept me coming back. It was knowing that there could be quality to my life. I did not know what that meant and had no idea what that was going to take to do it. Knowing that I can achieve this makes me happy. That is all there is to it. Simple."

The disease of addiction is paradoxical. Everything that appears to be one way is really quite another. The disease constructs a wall of confusion by creating this crazy hall-of-mirrors situation. Nearly everything an addicted person thinks is healthy is really unhealthy. Nearly everything an addicted person thinks is negative is quite the opposite.

Those close to an addicted person know that nearly everything an addict promises is surely not going to happen. The true, higher, healthy nature of the alcoholic or addict makes the promise, but the suffering mind and body of the afflicted person can rarely make good on it.

It is as if, in order to support Itself, addiction brings together an unhealthy persona within a person and then fine-tunes that persona to use all one's strengths to maintain Itself. The disease operates on the best of one's talents and natural gifts, not one's weaknesses. Having something take over your personality by utilizing all of your strengths would be amusing as a science fiction movie, but it is wickedly destructive when it is real life, and it is *your* life or the life of someone you care very much about.

Many of us wish to be free of the disease, so we enter into an outrageous struggle with It, justifying It, trying to control It, bargaining with It. An obvious example is when alcoholics or addicts promise themselves to have only one drink or drug dose at a certain time or to limit their substance to a certain number under specific circumstances. The more we try to be free of the disease, the further in Its grip we become. It is as if struggling against the disease brings us to the final phase of destruction sooner than if we had not tried to break out of It with our very best thinking.

Happiness Redefined

When we speak of finding a new freedom and a new happiness through recovery, what we mean is that our definition of happiness, as well as all of the actions that support this new happiness, change. If we insist on clinging to old definitions of freedom and happiness, we are also stuck with old behaviors that keep us from experiencing it. And it should come as no surprise that all of our old behaviors have that well-developed persona—addiction—enmeshed and grown through with it.

Old definitions include such ideas as always having to be defensive, vigilant, protected, on guard, judgmental, and suspicious because the addict/alcoholic world is seen as offensive, untrustworthy, unsafe, and attacking. Recovery brings an opportunity for an entirely new world perception, and, as if by magic, once perception changes, the world seems to cooperate quite nicely. It does not take long before all that mental, physical, emotional, and spiritual energy is used to enjoy a supportive, nurturing, responsive, and safe world instead of its opposite.

The type of new happiness that recovery brings is unique to each individual. Some people recognize this after a brief period of sobriety and some take longer. One person said that he felt the very first inklings of a new freedom when he could pass by a liquor store and realize that he had no attachment or need for it any longer. He used to obsess about his stock of booze hidden around his home whenever he passed the liquor store on his way to and from work. To be free of the requirement to do this is definitely a new freedom.

Another person experiences happiness in recovery as having a sense of independence and autonomy that she had never before experienced. After five years of sobriety, she realized that her view of happiness was limited and that she was in charge of inventing that definition for herself. It was her definition, and therefore when she felt happiness, that belonged to her as well. Nothing and nobody else was in charge. She had just as much choice, now sober, to choose what expanded or limited her happiness, so most of the time, she chose not to limit it at all.

To review the First Promise of Sobriety:

~Freedom and happiness are not optional or randomly given gifts. They are a birthright.

~The need for freedom is fundamental to our nature as human beings.

~Having a sense of freedom is so important to sobriety that it is the First of the Twelve Promises.

~The loss of freedom (i.e., powerlessness) is addressed in the First of the Twelve Steps of Alcoholics Anonymous and answered by the First of the Twelve Promises.

~There are many ways to experience this new freedom and new happiness, some large, some small.

~Happiness and freedom begin to develop the moment we decide to get and stay sober.

~Happiness and freedom are developing in our lives once we are sober even before we are able to appreciate these fully.

~Freedom and happiness are defined by each person.

CHAPTER TWO

PROM #2 We Will Not Regret the Past
nor Wish to Shut the Door on It

*I will bring myself to a place of willingness to stop running
from the past so that I can begin to grow into my own
serenity, peace, and wisdom.*

In the first chapter, we learned that the disease of addiction does
several things to us in much the same way that a dictator takes
over an entire country. Of all that It does, It accomplishes three
primary goals with great efficiency. This disease

1. negatively impacts our ability to perceive ourselves accurately.
2. disconnects us from having heartfelt, meaningful relationships with others.
3. renders us incapable of trusting any power greater than ourselves, resulting in spiritual disconnection.

Let's begin by looking at the first item on this list. (The second
and third items will be discussed in chapters 4 and 11.) We look
at our past and present actions and believe they are justifiable
and, overall, right. With our diminished ability to see ourselves
clearly, the disease is free to continue and progress in Its ugly,
quiet way.

When we look to the actions of our past, we think we have
taken right action when we may not have done this at all. We
think we were right when we were not. Addiction allows us to
look at our past and justify, overlook, or minimize our patterns
of negative behavior. When It does this, It creates a false reality.
We cannot help but react to this reality as if it is the truth. It
appears to be the truth. But addiction has skewed the truth to
mask Its tracks.

When there is no problem, there is no need for a solution. This
is the strategy that addiction uses. If we cannot see ourselves as

addicted, then why should we stop drugging and drinking? Again, this disease has been called cunning, baffling, and powerful. What could be more cunning than erasing from our view the very problem that, if we knew of its existence, we would begin resolving? The very fact that we doubt what others are telling us about our drinking or drugging proves that the disease has gained power over us.

Perhaps the most hideous aspect of addictive disease is that It uses our very own strengths, made of our intelligence and talents, to usurp us. It is clever in that, in this case, It prevents us from looking clearly into the past in order to preserve Itself in our present and guarantee Itself a future. Is there any science fiction thriller that presents an alien enemy more horrible than this? A disease that evilly toys with the way we see the world so that we, by our actions, negatively impact the world is the type of plot that belongs in a thriller novel and not in our reality.

Seeing the Past Clearly

This clever feature of addictive disease prevents us from enjoying oversight of ourselves with any positive result. It also prevents us from having hindsight. Our perception of our history is altered while we, or those we care about, are under the influence of mood-altering substances. With addiction, hindsight is *not,* as the saying goes, 20/20.

Hindsight, or our ability to see our past clearly, is a learning function that, when damaged through the use of alcohol or drugs, renders us unable to look at the past to guide ourselves through the present and into the future. Without this ability, we cannot learn from our mistakes. We cannot clean up the wreckage of our actions. We are locked into a cycle of repeating the same thing over and over again, expecting different results. This is commonly known as the definition of insanity.

> The definition of insanity: Insanity is
> repeating the same actions over and over
> again while expecting different results.

The Second Promise of Sobriety says that, "We will not regret the past nor wish to shut the door on it." It strongly tells us that the prize for remaining sober is true awareness *as it is,* not as we would like it to be. Learning and change will result from this gift. The insanity of the disease will go into remission and a sense of sanity will take its place. This is a lofty Promise that is, at first, difficult to believe.

 Being able to look into the past and gain understanding from it is a gift of sobriety. When we give up the shame and guilt that is a by-product of addictive behavior, we are free to open up the door to the past. We can then rely on our own experience to help us know the healthy way to go in the present. Being able to look behind us from whence we came helps us judge how relatively right or wrong we are in this very day.

While addicted to alcohol or drugs, we can look into the past, but not with a clear mind and an open heart. We peer at it with fear and loathing. We have developed self-victimizing patterns thanks to not being able to learn from our mistakes. Then we have perfected these behaviors over time. To look at the past only seems to make us feel worse. When we feel worse, we need relief from the feeling. We drink or use again. It is less and less effective. The disease closes in until we feel that desperate sense of hopelessness. Often, if It closes in enough, if we feel desperate enough, we will go to any lengths to escape the cycle. And often, thank goodness, this means giving up the addictive substance. Hopefully at this point, we are thinking of getting help so that we don't have to go through this difficult process alone, as it can sometimes be physically dangerous. Many understand this final desperate willingness to go to any lengths to alleviate the utter hopelessness as "hitting bottom."

The moment we give up our addictive substance, healing begins. First, and often uncomfortably so, it begins on a physical level. Our bodies need to cleanse away the toxins. Next, we begin to undergo a profound change in our brain chemistry. It is in this area where the Second Promise of Sobriety begins to become noticeable. For some it occurs immediately; for others, it slowly emerges sometime between six months and three years after we become abstinent. This is when the gift of hindsight begins to assist us in growth and change.

Embracing the Gray Area

When we are using or drinking, an "all-or-nothing" or "black-and-white" way of thinking develops to help maintain the cycle of the disease. When we become abstinent, we regain something very precious that we need in order to improve our lives: Let us call this precious state of being "gray area."

Gray area develops when we stop ingesting mood-altering substances because the natural state for most of us, without changing our perception, is to appreciate gradations of life. It is natural to perceive some things as slightly bad or slightly good. This is normal and necessary for everyday living and growth. As we gain wisdom and health, we can go further and remove "good" and "bad" labels altogether. But for now, seeing the finer levels between somewhat good and somewhat bad is just fine. Sobriety brings a healing in this area. The gradations between black and white slowly return. Gray is restored to us in small increments. Problems are not all bad, perceived at the same level of extremity as they were when we were drinking or using. By the same token, pleasures are not all good to the same degree. And, as regards this particular Promise, when we look into the past, we can see with greater clarity that we ourselves were not all good or all bad. We can see the choices we made, the patterns we participated in, the areas where we became stuck, and the moments of clarity when we were able to move forward.

The all-or-nothing attitude of the addicted person begins to fade, often in increments too small to be easily detected. This Promise, that we will not regret the past, is connected to development of the gray area, because we are then able to begin recovery with those things of the past that we or our sponsor, mentor, or advisor feels that we can handle. Gray area reduces small things to small things. Remember that the disease of addiction impacts our perception and in our all-or-nothing state, we see most problems as incredibly huge when, in reality, some may be major and some may not be quite as difficult to deal with. Not dealing with any of them because all problems falsely appear to be unworkable creates a mountain of chaos. *Chaos is the outcome of the insanity of the disease of addiction.*

Since problems and circumstances are not all good or all bad, we have choices as to where to begin our new lives. We may not yet be able to make the changes, but we are able to become *willing* to make changes. It certainly helps to choose the lighter, less frightening places in our past as starting points for growth and change. It is easier to be willing to move forward when we can see the gray in life. The Second Promise of Sobriety grants us this gift often before we are aware that we have the ability to use it. The more days of sobriety we have, the easier the starting point of this gift is to see.

Being able to see the gray in life, or the gradations between black and white, between extremes in thought and action, is something that begins to happen as our sanity is restored. Recall in the first chapter the comparison between Step One of the Twelve Steps of Alcoholics Anonymous and the First Promise of Sobriety in the Big Book. The two were symbiotic, stating the path (in the Step) and then stating the destination (in the Promise).

Similarly, Step Two contains a path and a destination for our journey toward attaining the Promises of Sobriety. The Second Step of AA states that we "Came to believe that a Power greater than ourselves could restore us to sanity." The words to keep in mind when thinking about the link between the Second Step and the Second Promise are "Came to believe." Recall the discussion about gray area earlier in this chapter. You learned that when we are active in our addiction, we often participate in all-or-nothing types of thinking, also called black-and-white thinking. With this type of thinking, thoughts are extreme, and reactions to our thoughts and perceptions are equally extreme. This helps to create chaos and insanity. With extreme thoughts, we react in extreme ways over and over again, repeating our behaviors whether they are effective or not. This is the definition of insanity.

The words "Came to believe" are important here, when thinking about the Second Promise, because once the insanity of all-or-nothing thinking stops, we can look clearly at the past and our behaviors and learn from them. We see that things are not black or white or all good or all bad. The Second Step says that we "Came to believe," not that "We believe" or "We had our sanity restored." It talks about a gradual process that involves gray area and the ability to learn new behaviors.

The Higher Power Connection

For many people the concept of any sort of Higher Power either never existed for them or disappeared along the road of disappointments, traumas, and addictive behaviors. Creating a Higher Power connection, understanding, or reconnection is something that often occurs gradually, very much like the gray area discussed above. Without sobriety, there can be no gray area. Without gray area, there can be no looking back to find what has been missing along the way. Without our past, there can be no learning. We are able to gradually create or re-create a Higher Power concept so that we can better handle looking back on our past without regret and without wishing to shut the door on it.

Being able to live in the present, now sober, having the healing that comes from a clear, clean mental state allows us to do miraculous things with our consciousness. In the world of today, we are given the potential for an incredible level of awareness, or ability to be highly conscious about even the smallest of things, because this is how we make our individual contribution to the world. Our full presence is asked for and, sober, we are able to respond with a clear mind.

In our addicted state, our brains are acting and reacting to substances, not to our real environment. We are playing God with our sense of reality, with our consciousness and our lack thereof. We are still under the ruse of the cunning, baffling, and powerful disease of addiction. We can only see what It allows us to see. To protect Itself, It creates a black-and-white world, an either/or existence. We aren't reacting to true reality, yet we believe that we are. We cannot learn, as our minds are sheltered from gaining new experience. They are too busy protecting the disease to do anything else.

Often, the past is fraught with pain. Since we cannot deal with such feelings in a healthy way, we play God and block our feelings connected to this pain with chemicals. And the more we do this with drugs and alcohol, the more pain we associate with our past. Then the less we want to go there and the more we want not to be anywhere but where it doesn't feel bad.

The Second Promise reflects the destination set out by the Second Step of AA. Now that we have stopped playing God, and have begun to accept that we cannot heal by ourselves, the positive process of learning to look into our past and not shut the door on it has begun. We begin to realize that we are connected to something greater and more powerful than ourselves. It becomes safer to look back while feeling supported in this way. Looking back gives us perspective. It gives us depth. It allows us to learn from past behavior and experiences. It is corrective and transforming. This enriches the present and makes it even more precious than it already is.

We can calibrate our actions and recalibrate them based on a rich store of information. Fortunately, one of the gifts of sobriety is that eventually, hindsight and accurate objectivity are gradually restored if the disease has not progressed too far. We are then better able to take responsibility for our own behavior and pull from the past not only negative experiences, but positive ones as well.

There is great pride and dignity in one's own ability to self-regulate. Addictive disease decreases a person's self-worth and sense of dignity. The gift of being able to look the past squarely in the eye and not spit at it or run from it is well worth the struggle to remain sober. Everybody deserves to feel good about who he or she is, and everybody is entitled to this particular gift.

Without looking into the past, we cannot forgive ourselves and others. If we cannot get a clear view, despite the pain that we might feel, of what we did to ourselves and others as a result of the disease of addiction, we can never take an inventory of that damaged way of life. We can never become accountable for our behavior. We can never make amends for the pain that we have caused, and we will never be free of that pain ourselves. The Second Promise of Sobriety becomes even more important when it is clear that it promises relief from this pain.

The Miracle of Accountability

Looking into the past is essential, for with the clarity and perspective that the past can bring comes spiritual awakening and sanity. With sanity comes healing and learning. And with healing and learning comes growth, connection, and then all the rest of the gifts of sobriety can follow. That is why we would not wish to shut the door on the past even when this Second Promise begins to come true. We can see the light in the faces of our loved ones as we reconnect to the world. We can feel the light in our own selves as we become accountable for our actions.

The Second Promise of Sobriety brings with it a miracle. Accountability feels good. Sanity feels good. At an AA meeting recently, the speaker shared that his sponsor had once told him something that had finally begun to come true for him. He said, "Now that I am sober, I'm not having such incredible highs and lows, but I am feeling reasonably good nearly all the time."

To look into the past brings perspective and light. To give up playing God all alone in an unfriendly universe is to lighten one's load a million-fold. Here is how one fellow expressed the sense of joy he felt about this particular gift:

"The miracle here is that I am now accountable for my actions. I want to die with dignity and I want a gravestone that says, simply, 'He was accountable.' That's it. In other words, the miracle is that now, if I tell you that a chicken can pull a freight train, you should immediately go out and look for a harness."

Getting sober means, for many, *learning to use pain for growth*. It also means having the ability and willingness to bring character defects into the open. Being sober means being able to admit these defects to ourselves and others. We can become willing to have the burden of these defects lifted from us. We can become willing to recognize when we are no longer struggling with the shame and guilt from our past behavior, a struggle that prevents us from enjoying the present moment. With sobriety, we receive the gift of relief because we realize that we are not bad people, but simply people with a disease that needs to be managed. The second gift of sobriety is multifaceted and this particular advantage is just one of the many shining sides of this second gem.

Making Amends

In the following story, a man in recovery shares an excellent learning experience that came from this very gift of sobriety. Through hindsight, he was able to see what he had done, make amends, and then enjoy the experience of relief. This gift continued to guide him through further challenges, because once he knew how good it felt to live honestly and with integrity, when given a choice one more time, he knew exactly what to do. He had been able, thanks to the gift of the Second Promise of Sobriety, to use his past to guide his present.

"When I got sober, I was still facing the wreckage of my past, was aware that I needed to make amends, and was overwhelmed. I just didn't see how I could ever get past it. I started right away cleaning it up. I read about Dr. Bob who started, as they say in the book, mending fences right away. He didn't do a Fourth or Fifth Step, but he went on to do a Ninth Step like on his first day![1] I knew that if I didn't do something like that, like clean up some of that crap, that I wouldn't make it. I wouldn't even make it to the Fourth Step. So I got into my vehicle and went to Colorado and made amends to my kids. I had all four of them sitting down, told them the whole story, made my amends, and felt immensely relieved.

"A few months later I had occasion to go out on leave to Colorado where my parents and stepfather live. I sat down with them and I was going to do the Ninth Step with them, but they couldn't hear it. It brought up so much pain for them and all that they could say was, 'Oh my, we don't need to talk about that. That's old stuff.' I tried to explain what it was about and

---

1. There are Twelve Steps in the program of Alcoholic Anonymous. The Fourth Step is that we "Made a searching and fearless moral inventory of ourselves." The Fifth Step is "Admitted to God, to ourselves, and to another human being the exact nature of our wrongs." The Ninth Step is "Made direct amends to such people wherever possible, except when to do so would injure them or others."

they didn't want to hear it. So I came back to California and put it in a letter and sent it and did it that way. I made amends to my former in-laws and my first wife, and the relief was immense. I felt good about myself; I wasn't living in all that fear. I stopped looking over my shoulder.

"Then, and this was way before I even got through even so much as half of the Twelve Steps, I relapsed. I got a DUI. When I went to court, the judge said, 'How do you plead?' I said, 'Guilty.' I had been going to a meeting every day, sometimes two during that thirty-day period before I slipped. So when I got in front of the judge, I really didn't care what they did. They could have sent me to San Quentin. I was willing to pay whatever price I had to pay. I was starting to get it about honesty and not leaving a trail of lies behind me. I felt so good."

We have to be able to look at the past in order to let go of it. Looking at the past allows us to not only learn about the social world and how to be in it, but also learn about ourselves and how to let others enjoy us. When we are free, through sobriety, to know ourselves and how we came to be blessed with this newfound sense of self, we are free to share what and who we are with others. We are also free to perceive love and all the healthy forms that it can take. We know that we are being cared for as our real selves, as the sum total of our past and present.

Without growth, we are stuck in a farce that plays itself out over and over, wearing us down. We scratch our heads each time the farce replays itself, whether it be a job, a relationship, or some other conflictual issue. Growth comes from looking clearly and freely at the past, objectively making an assessment as to what occurred through our past actions, and then taking action to create the more desirable outcome. Our sobriety gives us the opportunity to regain the basic ability to do this, but it is our recovery that provides us with the means to carry it out.

Being in recovery means having the willingness to stop running from emotional pain. It means that now we use this pain to learn, change, and grow into our fullest potential. Pain ceases to victimize us and begins to become our teacher.

A wise old-timer once said that "no great positive change ever occurred to a person without first an experience of chaos followed by some degree of pain." The chaos is the disruption that is created when the status quo is broken or when an old habit can no longer exist due to behavior change. Some degree of pain follows the chaos, as the readjustment to the new order settles in. This type of pain is never long-lived. It is transitional in nature. Even when it seems not to be, it is temporary.

Living in the Present

Emotional growing pains are never equal to the fear they generate. To walk through and past the fear and into the reality is often the most healing thing a person can do at the start of the recovery journey. To do it alone, without a map and with no clue as to what the destination looks like, is unthinkably insane. The Twelve Steps can be seen as a suggestion of a map, and the Twelve Promises can be seen as a suggestion of the destination.

Living in the past is not what is being implied here, nor is living in the future an option for people in recovery. What recovery and treatment programs teach us to do is stay in the present, in the here and now. That is where love exists. That is where peace, serenity, and pleasure exist. Living in the past or the future only brings disappointment and anxiety. But being able to "not regret the past nor wish to shut the door on it" and then acting in the present to effect change does a great deal to determine what will occur in the future while we are living in the present. This means that we are creating our future in the present by utilizing our past. What is better than to take a victimizing, painful past and transform it by our own willingness into something that empowers us and teaches us how to experience ourselves and others positively?

The gift of hindsight enhances our enjoyment of this very moment. Following, another woman in recovery describes her experience of this particular gift; she sees it as a God-given and God-directed event that she follows. Her lack of struggle with her own ego needs and her willingness to take care of her emotional business signifies the mark of a person who is said to be "working a good program." She came to believe that a power greater than herself could restore her to sanity. This belief was then followed by the Promise of being able to go back and mend fences.

"I believe that God allowed me to have my children for a few years and I've done a fairly good job with that. I have mended my relationships with my parents and my sister. I feel like I have fulfilled what it is that He wanted me to do. If there is more that He wants me to do, then He's going to have to tell me what it is because I don't know what it is, and I'm perfectly willing to listen and follow direction. To be of service to others, as AA says, is what I feel that God put me here for and that's what I'm doing. So I'm ready to go whenever He wants me to go. If it weren't for the Promises of Alcoholics Anonymous coming true for me, if it weren't for being able to leave the door to the past open and talk with you about my history, you and I would have nothing to talk about, would we?"

Forgiving Ourselves and Others

Here is a story from another woman that goes further into detail about the meaning of enjoying the Second Promise of Sobriety. Several very painful events from the past combine to beat down her sense of self, her self-esteem, her ability to love and be loved. The gift of hindsight allows this woman to look into her past carefully, learn from it, let go of baggage, and move on to a healthier way of living where love, serenity, and peace can exist for her.

"All of the Promises in the Big Book began coming true for me at about year ten of my recovery from drug addiction. The door to the past was now wide open and I could go back and look there, see the painful events, and understand that I had been an innocent child and nothing more or less. I did not create that ugly world of my youth. I had been powerless to fix it then as much as I am powerless to change its course now except by my own individual actions here and now.

"One of the most pleasurable Promises came true when my spiritual program began focusing on forgiveness and freedom from desire. I dedicated three years to walking to and from my office, saying a prayer of forgiveness for each and every single person that I harbored a resentment over, for myself and all the wrong things that I had done and harm that I had caused in the past. I looked at it, acknowledged the reality of it, and then forgave myself and others. I did this over and over, day in and day out, once in the morning and once in the evening, year after year after year.

"I had purchased a pair of heavy hiking shoes to do these meditation/prayer walks (three miles a day), and at year three had worn holes through the leather heel and sole even though there were many inches of leather and rubber to wear through. The shoes were a terrific symbol of what I had thought was the impenetrable shell protecting my wounded spirit. By the time the shoes were useless, transparent in some places and often even harmful to wear, I noted with a start of surprise one spring day that I simply had no more hatred inside of me. I forgave my family and every single person who I felt had harmed me in any way, large or small. Then I forgave myself for each and every injury of any type that I had caused myself and the world, physical or not, intended or otherwise.

"This is how the Second Promise of Sobriety brought me such gifts. My spirit was freed of the weight of anger and resentment in the past, allowing me to feel unburdened and happy in the present. I no longer live in the past, therefore I no longer relive the past in the present. I feel limitless as for what I can do with my life, instead of limited by my past circumstances. I feel worthy of receiving love and have a lot of love to give. That one single Promise of Sobriety, 'We will no longer regret the past nor wish to shut the door on it,' has brought me the greatest joy and hope each and every day. It began happening the moment that my belief system shifted from me ruling the universe to me fitting into it, interacting with others, held in the arms of a Higher Power. I was able to begin working the Second Step of AA as soon as I became willing and able to change through staying sober and being able to look into the past with clarity. From there it evolved to where it is now, and my relief and gratitude for this Promise coming true for me are immense."

To review the Second Promise of Sobriety:

~ Sobriety initiates a return of gray area so that we can see gradations of things and get rid of all-or-nothing or black-and-white types of thinking.

~ Being able to look into our past with accurate perception allows us to make changes, to learn and grow.

~ We can see how our past was absolutely necessary in order for us to arrive at this place of gratitude and hope in the present.

~ Leaving the door to the past open, we can forgive ourselves and make amends to others for wrongs we have done and leave in the past our shame, embarrassment, and guilt.

~ Traumas that belong in the past stay in the past and are not automatically relived in the present thanks to the healing process.

~ The Second Promise of Sobriety helps us enjoy a sense of accountability.

~ The Second Step of Alcoholics Anonymous is addressed by the Second Promise of Sobriety.

PROM 3 + 4
CHAPTER THREE

3) We Will Comprehend the Word Serenity,
4) and We Will Know Peace

Please help me to stop trying so hard to find serenity. Deep inside myself I know that it is sitting there, waiting for me to join with it. I no longer need to struggle to get it. It is my birthright to have.

Is there any more perfect example of chaos than our addiction? Our addiction feels like a tornado, gaining in force and fooling those who are staying in the eye of the storm into believing that everything is "just fine." We medicate ourselves and stay in the eye of the storm as long as we possibly can. Outside of the eye, family members are swirling, trying to find their own sense and peace in the maelstrom. Our family members and loved ones take on roles that hold them in a place that they would not necessarily choose consciously. But nonetheless, this place is familiar, routine, and well known to them, and, therefore, safe.

Think of this safe, comfortable place as a job description. Each of us holds our own job description in a family, and each job is interdependent upon another person's job. Should one person fail to do his or her job well, or cease performing the job duties (whether it is positive or negative in nature), it causes great distress and threatens an eventual reorganization. A family reorganization is feared because things were familiar and strangely comfortable as they were. Change would break apart the comfortable, well-known pattern. Addicts, alcoholics, and those who are emotionally involved with them really dislike change, even though they may constantly profess to want reform. The cycle of this disease is so strong that it can cause a family to fear the very change it knows must happen. It is not unusual to see family members sabotaging progress toward healthy change just to have one more day of false serenity.

As long as we hold our job description as chief addict/alcoholic, our family members may continue to keep their job descriptions, as chief caretaker, master distracter, major savior, expert disappearing act, and so on. All family members are held in place in this way, around our job description, because in any organization, including a family organization, the energy usually goes toward the weak, not the strong. The chief addict/alcoholic role is powerful because the family needs to rally around the chaos and illness it creates in order to keep appearing or feeling as though it has some kind of equilibrium or balance. The family is held in place by some invisible, negative glue until it begins its reorganization, which can also be known as recovery.

Truth makes itself known first to the soul; therefore the family, made up of a group of truthful souls, lives a lie that is often too difficult to admit to. The false sense of serenity that is periodically gained in this way is a facade. And it hurts every single friend and family member not to live authentically. It especially hurts *us*. For we are, almost by definition, the ones who need the most armor and protection because our spirits are so soft. When we reach for that drink or drug, we reach for our armor. In doing so, we create the tornado that catches our loved ones and would have us feeling even worse for the shame and the guilt that our disease causes.

Genuine Serenity Is Possible

Serenity is a birthright. Although our disease has masked it from us, serenity is entirely obtainable. Making the changes necessary to live a lifestyle of recovery takes an incredible amount of commitment and courage. It is this lifestyle that creates the real serenity. The authentic sense of internal peace that radiates from us, just like ripples in a pond, must eventually spread outward and impact all other inhabitants of the pond. In this case, of course, the inhabitants of the proverbial pond are the people close to us for whom we care the most. We can't deliberately change them, and they can't deliberately reach out and change us without using a considerable amount of force or leverage. But we are the ones afflicted with a cunning, baffling, and powerful disease, and it is most empowering if we become willing to take responsibility for our actions that were caused by the disease. By taking deliberate Steps to put this disease in remission, we cannot help but create a world of genuine serenity around us. And when does real serenity begin? It begins the first moment we take the first positive action.

Would you like to know what this addiction is all about? It is contained in a single word: *paradox.* The dictionary says that a paradox is a statement that is contrary to common belief. A statement that seems contradictory, unbelievable, or absurd, but that may actually be true in fact. What this disease does to us and to those around us is create a "looking glass" phenomenon. What we want and what we work for while we are active in our addiction creates exactly the opposite outcome of our intentions. The harder we work, the further away the outcome seems to be. It's easy to understand the concept of paradox by envisioning a picture of a gerbil wheel. If the point is to get somewhere, the faster you run on the wheel, the more work you do. More often than not, no ground is covered at all.

This is the truth about our disease, especially as it relates to serenity. Some people spend their entire lives trying to obtain serenity and peace. While we are active in our addiction, we think we've got it made. Serenity and peace seemingly can be created in a very short period of time by a drink or a drug. For every false moment of serenity and peace that this method provides us, days, months, and often years of our lives are extracted in anxious payment for same. In other words, those moments of real internal quietude that were coming to us as our natural birthright are spent forever, moment by moment, replaced with a lesser and more temporary version that carries with it tremendous debt. Real serenity and peace cost us nothing in the way of money, stress, or strain on relationships. It just is what it is. False serenity and peace cost us dearly. Often, they cost us our very lives.

While we are active in our addiction, attempting to achieve serenity, serenity is the furthest from us that it can possibly be. A false sense of serenity is not only temporary, it is also unbelievable because we know deep down that it is falsely achieved.

Just the fact that we are attempting to achieve serenity pushes it away from us. Thanks to the paradox of the disease of addiction, whatever we usually believe is necessary in order to achieve serenity is way off the mark. Often, the last thing we would believe about feeling a sense of serenity is that it is easily and readily obtainable. The lifestyle that goes with addictive disease appears to be an easy one at first, but winds up being chaotically difficult. The lifestyle that appears to go well with serenity and peace appears to require difficult steps but turns out to be the simplest thing in the world.

Because of this inside-out type of thinking, it seems easy to justify avoiding the change that would bring serenity and peace. Therefore, we avoid these changes, and the disease wins in Its cunning, baffling, and powerful way. If this paradox weren't so deadly, it would be incredibly amusing. In AA meetings with those who have been clean and sober long enough to appreciate all of the gifts of sobriety, you will sometimes hear the grateful laughter that comes from escaping the confounding paradox of this disease just one more day.

The Paradox of Intellect

Overall, we are a highly gifted bunch. We must use our intellect. And because we so often use it in the service of our addiction, we perfect its ability to protect the disease. It is not unusual to find extremely bright, gifted, and high-functioning individuals in early recovery programs.

It is as if there is a petri dish inside of us that requires the right kind of nutrients in order to grow the disease. It just so happens that our very own intellect provides the right kind of disease-growing nutrients. It should not surprise us that the disease quickly uses our intellect against us to grow Itself. And it is, paradoxically, our own intellect that prevents us from seeing the simplicity built right in to experiencing serenity and real peace.

It is not that we have to wipe out our fantastic-thinking function in order to find peace (although many of us actually manage to do this via drug- or alcohol-promoted brain damage), it is that we need to find a new way to look at the world when we finally decide to become clean and sober. Our sobriety buys us this ability. The ability to act upon our feelings rather than our intellect is obtainable with practice. It is our intellect that helps to support the tornado of chaos that holds serenity off in the distance.

Our feelings, which begin to become available to us once we are sober, help cut through the difficulties that inappropriate use of our intellect can create. Our feelings may seem to have the power to rise up and overwhelm us, cause us to feel suffocated or buried under too much emotion, but this is just another sad trick of the disease itself. The reality is that even the worst of our feelings, or all of them jumbled together, can do us less harm than using mood-altering substances.

Sobriety repairs our ability for self-insight. It allows us singular moments of clarity with which to see beyond what our intellectual mind, so well developed through our addiction, has allowed us to see. Beyond the narrow confines of our intellectual hindsight is a world that is unscrambled. Flipped backward upon itself—turned inside out—that world is one where those of us who are clean and sober must live. That is where the Third Promise, "We will know serenity and we will know peace" begins to happen.

The Serenity Quest

Here is a story from a well-traveled, extremely gifted man whose sobriety spans nearly five decades. See if, in his story, you can find any similarities in your own quest for serenity and peace.

"Let's say I'm looking for serenity, searching for it. I've got to stay un-serene so that I can continue to search for it. Trying to find peace is the very thing that keeps it away. Now it is the same thing with sobriety. A person comes in and says, 'God Almighty! I've come to AA fifteen times. I've tried to stay sober and I just can't make it!' Then we often say, just casually, 'Well then, don't try so hard.'

"But here is the point: As long as you try to stay sober, you've got to stay drunk so that you can continue to try to stay sober.

"I was invited to go to Asia to work some time ago. I figured as long as I was going there, and with my curiosity about Eastern religions, I'd look into their belief system for anything that would help the recovering addict and alcoholic. Once I got there, they had a lot of rest and relaxation periods for us because it is so hot that most Western people can't stand it. But not me. I went out and learned about Hinduism and Buddhism, Taoism and Confucianism, and so forth. I spent a long time in India, Indonesia, Singapore, and Hong Kong. Later, I came back and spent almost a year in Nepal. Well! I was driving to try and find something about serenity and peace. Here is one of many instances.

"I was in an ashram in a commune run by a famous Sri, or 'saint' named Sri Ramana Maharishi. I was there at the time of Dewali, which is very much like our Easter celebration, as it is a time of renewal and rebirth. There were about 150 East Indian people and I was the only visitor there. I wore a doti, which is a sheet that goes down to your feet and you tie it up around your waist sort of like a diaper. If you have seen pictures of Gandhi, then you can visualize what this garment looks like.

"For Dewali, we were awakened at about two in the morning and herded into a great big courtyard. In that courtyard there were platforms supporting kettles that were heating the water and oil inside them. A fellow was on each platform, scooping out the water and giving it to each of us in a basin. After the basin was filled, we were given a new doti, told to go to a dressing room, wash our bodies with the oil and water mixture, and change into a fresh doti. This ashram was located at the foot of a mountain known as Arunachal. Arunachal in Hindi means sun. It is said that Rama, one of the many Hindu Gods, lives in that mountain. The leader told us that we were supposed to walk around the base of this mountain, which was about a ten-mile walk. We were instructed to call out 'Rama, Rama, Rama!' This was to be done frequently during the ten-mile walk. I got to the ninth mile and was so tired that I think I actually saw Rama come up and thumb his nose at me. Now that is the kind of stuff I was doing, month after month, to try and find serenity. I just was so determined to find it.

"Well! I finally came back to my little apartment after my travels and travails. I just lay there, collapsed from travel fatigue. My search was unsuccessful, I thought, and the trip was over. As I lay there, a strange thing began to happen to me. Slowly, the urge to find serenity and peace diminished and diminished some more and then . . . it thoroughly evaporated. As it did so, there behind it all was . . . serenity.

"It became apparent to me that it was the *search* that was the trouble. I was so busy looking for something in the future that I could not experience it in the present. Serenity and peace only exist right now. Recovery affords us the opportunity to experience just what 'now' feels like. Serenity, therefore, is a Promise fulfilled as one of the gifts of sobriety."

The *Tao Te Ching* provides us with an idea of how serenity can be obtained when one has an antiserenity disease such as ours. It says that not knowing something is the real definition of true knowledge. Admitting that we are sick allows us to take the first actions toward health. The one who is really in control realizes that he or she is actually not in control at all. This Eastern view of things is not unlike the Twelve Steps of AA at all. It is simply another way to view the same thing. What is so wonderful about working the Steps is that they were written specifically for viewing this one single phenomenon—addiction as It affects human beings. Other ways to view addiction may also be applicable and useful, but the one written specifically for the purpose of putting the disease of addiction in remission gets right to the heart of things.

Letting Go of Control

Sobriety offers us the clarity of mind to know that, in many instances, there will be no particular clarity of mind. Accepting this means embracing ambiguity and living with a sense of deep trust in the way things already are. Ambiguity and trust are the enemies of control. Those of us who have studied this disease understand that control is truly the master addiction.

Recall the metaphorical petri dish that was brought up earlier. Another ingredient in the petri dish of the disease is control. When we overutilize our intellectual function, we get a false sense of control that is unmanageable. A day-to-day lifestyle of recovery helps us to know a sense of spiritual connectedness. Spiritual connectedness allows us to relax and not try to control people, places, and things. The most important fact we can learn is that we cannot know everything, do everything, and control everything. Admitting defeat over the incredible task of knowing, doing, and controlling everything is extremely relieving.

In chapters 1 and 2, the Twelve Steps of Alcoholics Anonymous were described as markers on a road, pointing the way toward a particular destination. It was also noted that the Twelve Promises directly relate to every one of the Twelve Steps, assisting us creating an individualized picture in our own minds of our destination.

The Third Step of AA reads: "Made a decision to turn our will and our lives over to the care of God *as we understood Him.*" This Step points to the road marker on our journey to become clean and sober, telling us that using our self-will driven by our own intellect does not work. It tells us that we need to give that will to a power greater than ourselves. We may understand this power greater than ourselves to be another person, or perhaps a group of people. Now is the time to acknowledge that running our selves and our own lives, however we were initially taught to do it, doesn't work when we are afflicted with this disease. For us, the greatest work needs to be done right here, at the Third Step. Further growth cannot happen if we are going to hold fast to old belief systems about self-will and willpower.

The Third Promise, "We will comprehend the word serenity and we will know peace," correlates to the Third Step of AA in that if we take the road marker of the Third Step seriously and give up our will, turning it over to a power greater than ourselves, then serenity and peace will follow. When we come to that place where we can relax not knowing the who-what-when-where-and-why of all things around us, we have received yet another gift of sobriety. This is where serenity and peace come in.

Serenity is achieved after a simple yet deliberate set of changes have been made. The needed changes require looking at one's belief system that is built around this disease. Or, more aptly put, the disease that has wrapped itself like a strong weed around the very best belief systems. Ask yourself, "Is this belief system serving my sobriety?" If you answer no, then you must clearly decide to drop that belief system whether you have a replacement belief system or not! You will then be well on the way toward realizing the Third Promise.

The Serenity Prayer

One of the more common false beliefs carried into sobriety is that one has to try hard to achieve sobriety and try harder to reach the gifts that sobriety brings. The truth is that trying has nothing to do with achieving the gifts of sobriety. In fact, it is yet again another example of the paradox of this disease that the more you try to reach serenity, the further you move from achieving it and the more chaos you create while trying.

Perhaps this is why the Serenity Prayer is so popular with recovering addicts and alcoholics:

God, grant me the serenity
To accept the things I cannot change,
The courage to change the things I can,
And the wisdom to know the difference.

The very lifestyle of drug and alcohol addiction is anything but serene. Some people report getting a high or a thrill from obtaining their particular drug of choice. Some people are addicted to the thrill of their own lies. The game of not getting found out can also appeal to the addictive personality. Some people say that they were once actually attracted to the fast lifestyle with its riskiness and potential for danger. But eventually all people want to get their basic human needs met, and the body, mind, and spirit strive for serenity from a place deep in the core of each of us.

The quest for an exciting, fast lifestyle is a passing, more surface need. Recovery brings serenity, sometimes quickly and sometimes slowly, but for some it shows itself in moments of clarity, well before it is ever achieved. But when serenity is realized, it is one of the most important and precious gifts of sobriety. The woman who tells the following story still remembers this stunning event:

"I recall one particular day more than seventeen years ago, when I was sitting on a park bench one late afternoon, stoned out of my mind, paranoid that someone could tell how loaded I was, and depressed to the point of not being able to move my body. The depression was that heavy that I actually felt like I was carrying around lead shot in each leg and arm. I had been working a nowhere kind of job, the type of job that was not challenging, but more humiliating than anything else. The type of job that would suffocate a person if done long enough. I lived in a sloping, long-overdue-for-the-wrecking-ball type of clapboard house that had so many fleas in the carpet that nobody would visit me because the fleas would latch on to your ankles and make their way in circles up your legs.

"I had no friends. I kept my phone working in case I needed it to set up a dope deal, but otherwise it never rang. My life consisted of getting up, lighting up a joint, stuffing as much junk food into me as I could before heading up the street to this office where I filed three-by-five index cards in neat little rows for this guy all day long. Then it was time to walk home, blitz my brains out with whatever I happened to be able to get that night (I could never keep any sort of stash), and eventually collapse in a heap on an old sofa until morning.

"I was barely even twenty years old. I didn't know that others my age were going out on dates, seeing performances, attending concerts and parties where people actually talked with one another. That just wasn't my world. Vacations and family visits weren't part of my world either. My world was my couch, the walk to and from work, and that awful office with the job from hell. I never saw movies; I never listened to music. Occasionally I'd stare at the television, but it made no sense to me. My attention span was so poor back then that a half-hour sitcom couldn't even keep my attention no matter how I tried.

"You'd think I led the simple life, but it wasn't that way at all. On the contrary, there was no serenity in it whatsoever. My brain was useless except for the most routine of functions and sometimes that didn't include decent grooming habits. My body, for as young as it was, had become accustomed to doing very little, and so every day it felt like it wanted to do less and less. Given the chance, I'd lie on the couch day in and day out, using all of my sick-leave time up just so that I could stay loaded, out of it, with nothing to do but breathe and eat.

"The trouble was that even though I went to great lengths to put myself practically to sleep with all the drugs I did back then, my brain would not stop making me miserable. I felt awful about myself, guilty about all the millions of things I wasn't doing, even when I wasn't sure just what those specific things were, and absolutely ashamed of my behavior. I knew the difference between me a few years before that and me then, at that point. I didn't think it was normal to have to drag yourself out of bed and then do drugs to make yourself 'up' enough to drag yourself off to work. To say that I was depressed then was an understatement.

"So that day that I was sitting on a park bench, stoned, through the haze of my self-hatred and paranoia, through the weight of my depression, I had a single, extraordinary experience.

"The late-afternoon sunlight suddenly shot through the trees at a low angle; the light actually grew from the trees and made its way toward me. It illuminated me and surrounded me with reddish yellow streaks of light. The sight of this somehow shocked me out of being stoned. I had one long moment of clarity and with it, a sense of serenity. The light moved past me as the sun went down. Then it disappeared. I was no longer high, but the sense of the quietude in that moment, the clarity of thought, and the interest that I had in it stayed with me. I knew I would have to be straight in order to ever feel that way again. I was right. Being high made me feel crazy inside, made things more complicated than they ever could have been in reality. I spent so much time thinking my way through things when in fact it didn't take hours to ponder a thing, it took seconds.

"My sobriety brings me serenity in its simplicity. I no longer live like a pig as I did back then. I no longer have the kind of work that makes one think that dying would be better than filing index cards. My mind and body feel like they are working together, no longer against one another. I don't drag myself out of bed in the morning. I swing my legs out onto the floor and feel grateful for the clean flooring under my feet. I wonder what will happen to me today. What will be difficult, and what will be easy because I've gotten good at it. These aren't things a dope fiend thinks. But these are things that I do. Serenity to me is not having to work so hard all the time to do everyday simple things. I get the gift of serenity every day that I choose to stay clean from drugs."

The Serenity Prayer helps lay parameters for those of us who are still caught up in the opposite of achieving serenity, which is commonly known as control. A professional in recovery tells the following story:

"In order to move here I had to apply for a California license. The process was long and involved. I had to get a lot of records together in a certain period of time. It was frustrating to say the least and had it been another time, I would have gone off the wall. I had to fly over for an interview with this doctor, which turned out to be a real high point because we sat together and talked about recovery the whole time. It was a piece of cake. I tell the doctors here, 'Get sober. These things may happen.' And my wife recently remarked at how I just sort of flowed through that whole experience in a fairly serene manner. To some extent I guess that the Serenity Prayer played a big role in it. There were certain things I could do something about, and there were certain things about practicing in California that I couldn't do anything about."

So you see, the less this man tried to control his frustrating circumstances, the better he felt. The better he felt, the better the circumstances went and there began the unraveling of the disease. Those of us who are willing to let go of our incredible need to control are bound to experience the most sought-after, yet elusive gifts of sobriety: serenity and peace.

To review the Third Promise of Sobriety:

~Addiction creates chaos that impacts not only us but anyone we have connection with.

~Serenity is a birthright that positively impacts not only us but everyone we come into contact with.

~Addiction is paradoxical, creating an insane world where everything we do to achieve serenity and peace is undone by our own actions.

~We are gifted with ample intellect. The disease of addiction uses our own strengths to conquer us and keep us from our birthright of serenity.

~The Third Step of AA is a road marker in our journey toward realizing the Third Promise of serenity and peace.

CHAPTER FOUR

No Matter How Far Down the Scale We Have Gone, We Will See How Our Experience Can Benefit Others

I know that I have worth, both to others and to myself. Today I will take notice of even the smallest feeling of self-worth and value it more highly than ever before.

An earlier chapter described how the disease of addiction takes away our ability to see ourselves clearly, either in the present or in the past. The disease has another ugly facet: It has the ability to distance us from others. It does this because It needs to operate as freely as possible, uninterrupted by well-intentioned, caring people. These people are an enemy to the disease because they can clearly see that despite our protests, we are harming ourselves and other people with alcohol or drugs.

People who care about us the most have the most to lose if we self-destruct. They are the most prone to be brave in the face of their own shame and embarrassment. They are the ones who pull the veil from the face of the disease and expose It. Out of love and fear of loss, they are the ones who will be brave enough to speak the truth. Therefore, the disease causes us to slowly but surely distance ourselves from these very precious people. It twists our thinking so that we easily and logically find reasons to carry grudges, envy, resentments, and disappointments—reasons to cut these people out of our lives. Alone, we can be conquered. When we are connected to others in nonaddictive, healthy ways, it is more difficult for the disease to progress.

Recovery programs generally organize treatment into what is called a "therapeutic community." It is fairly well accepted by professionals specializing in drug and alcohol treatment that individual therapy is not generally as effective in treating addictions as this community or group-oriented method of treatment.

The program of Alcoholics Anonymous is also built around an idea of the healing power of a community of like-minded individuals. Because addiction causes a serious disconnection in our ability to relate to others, AA counteracts this disconnection with blind acceptance of the person who suffers from addictive disease. The friendly welcome, the repeated introductions, the embracing of visitors and newcomers, the lack of judgment, the tradition of opening AA membership to any person with a desire to be sober—all of these measures are taken to break the disease's ability to socially poison us.

The Punishment of Isolation

In ancient times, many different peoples of the world punished a serious offense by deeming the offender "invisible." Nobody in the tribe or clan was allowed to speak to that person ever again. Nobody could offer solace, food, or other-creature comfort. The person was turned out from the group, forced to leave and fend for himself or herself. There was no greater punishment for a human being than total isolation from others. The result was usually that the exiled, cutoff group member would die of one cause or another, unprotected, unloved, unsupported, lonely, and vulnerable to the elements.

In this regard, the differences between ancient times and present times are small. Exile proved an extreme punishment for a human being in ancient times, and death by exclusion is still one of the deepest forms of punishment there is. If the death is not the literal loss of life, than most certainly this type of punishment results in death by soul-killing.

It would not be going too far to say that addiction causes, in Its ability to separate an individual from his or her support group, a parallel form of soul-killing. Any social connection an addict or alcoholic is able to maintain becomes a false connection, thanks to the disease. Real words of affection and love are juxtaposed against a backdrop of lies, manipulations, excuses, and fruitless promises. It becomes difficult to separate truthful feelings of love from the facade of false words of love; thus begins the process of disconnection from one's community.

Those of us who are currently active in our addiction suffer just such a banishment. On top of disconnection from those around us, we have to find a way to deal with our feelings of shame and embarrassment because we are compelled to continue drinking or using drugs. It seems that we are bringing the worst down upon ourselves and we feel foolish. That is a hard thing to carry around all day, every day, so we try not to. The only way we know how to control feeling stupid and shameful is to disconnect from these feelings. We exile ourselves from our selves. We become emotionally, psychologically, spiritually, socially, and physically cut off from others. We try to keep up appearances and make it seem as if everything is fine, but it simply isn't.

As the disease of addiction progresses, the facade we've built fades away and soon the isolation from our community, from significant others, from spiritual connectedness, and from physical and emotional health is complete. Like the socially exiled offender of ancient times, we experience exposure to the elements, loneliness, and a sense of hopelessness as a result of this type of exile. As the isolation caused by the disease progresses, death becomes not a mere possibility, but an ironclad guarantee.

The Gift of Social Connection

Outpatient group therapy, therapeutic communities in treatment programs, and AA and other self-help groups are all testaments to the fact that *the antidote for addiction is social connection.* The disease easily evades helpful individuals, but it is so much more difficult for the disease to survive in a close-knit group.

It is not enough to merely show up at these group meetings, treatment services, or programs. As the following list illustrates, success through many treatment programs requires our undivided attention. The programs involve

1. sharing our experience, strength, and hope
2. telling the honest-to-goodness story of how we came to be at this turning point
3. unburdening ourselves
4. taking an inventory of ourselves based on reminders of the stories of others
5. being willing to listen to others and recognize our similarities, not our differences
6. hearing and seeing the disease operate in others whom we can identify with and feeling gratitude that we are well
7. helping others by being willing to share our own truth

All of these things, and more, serve to heal the addict/alcoholic. Reconnecting the person to his or her community and support system is the first and most important step in breaking the back of this disease. We do this by practicing a verbal version of the Fourth Step ("Made a searching and fearless moral inventory") in order to realize the Fourth Promise ("No matter how far down the scale we have gone, we will see how our experience can benefit others").

As Shakespeare wrote in *King Lear,* "Speak what we feel, not what we ought to say." Seeing "how our experience can benefit others" helps rebuild our self-esteem and decrease our shame and embarrassment. It is the actual process of practicing this form of communication about our real and true feelings, pleasant or unpleasant, that begins to provide us with the dignity that comes from being able to help others.

Therapists who work with alcoholics and addicts can tell you that a great many of their patients insist that they are "natural loners." Spending much of their time alone, doing solitary activities, not liking a lot of contact with others is considered a natural part of one's character. This trait is usually quite acceptable to them. But the professional sees that isolation and distancing from others is how the disease fells its hosts. The adage "Divide and conquer" does not only work in wartime; it works just as well biologically, psychologically, and emotionally when used to describe how the disease of addiction slowly but surely brings down its victims, and often anyone closely involved, by re-creating that ancient form of punishment: community exile.

The Benefits of Fellowship

After establishing complete abstinence from all mood-altering substances, reconnecting with others is perhaps the single most helpful part of the healing process from addictive disease. There are many ways to do this. The most popular and effective way is to actively participate in a Twelve Step or similar self-help program. Creating a sense of heartfelt fellowship with others who are going through similar struggles with the same disease is connecting. Entering a treatment program that emphasizes connection with a group of other alcoholics or addicts as its major therapeutic component is a good way to begin reconnecting and sharing.

Like community exile, sharing one's experience with others as a healing process goes back a long way. In ancient times, before experiences could be written down on paper, people shared their experiences, good and bad, and helped to alleviate their anxieties and fears by talking about them.

The Fourth Promise says, "No matter how far down the scale we have gone, we will see how our experience can benefit others." The great benefit in sharing one's story with others is that doing so raises the self-esteem of the person sharing, brings hope to the one listening, and breaks the isolation separating the speaker and the listener. The subject matter opens the heart, creating a sense of belonging. All people who share their personal stories, regardless of the consequences and effects of their addictive disease, help others as well as themselves.

Here, a recovering woman describes this process of sharing her experience with others:

"At first I thought the problem was just the way that I was made. Quiet, a loner. Never fit in with others. Didn't have much to say. Didn't feel like I was important enough to be heard. When I did speak to others, I didn't feel heard. When I went to a meeting, I'd arrive late and sit in the back. I'd leave quickly. I resented people who seemed to speak with others easily. And I was embarrassed to tell my story to anyone. It seemed worse than what anybody else had done. I didn't want to be known by what I had done before, but I couldn't get away from my own self! So gradually I made myself get there on time, then speak, even if just a bit, then stay for an extra minute or two afterward.

"Slowly but surely my ears opened up and I heard other people saying things that I could understand, and I then was able to get over my shame and share more of myself with others. I am still coming out of my shell, really, but I can see that I've come a long way. Sometimes the only thing that gets me to speak up is knowing that someone else will get something good from what I say. I feel like I belong to something, finally, and that there are people like me wherever I go.

"I feel proud of how far I've come and proud of those I've helped by opening up my heart to them. I guess you could say that this is what the Fourth Promise of Sobriety is all about."

Children growing up in the dysfunctional family systems caused by addiction learn this teaching: *Don't think, don't speak, and don't feel.* The Fourth Promise tells us that by entering a journey of self-revealing honesty, we not only engage in thinking, but also feeling. To top it all off, we break the most important dysfunctional family taboo: We feel. It is easy to see how the Fourth Promise is the antidote to this most destructive, inaccurate silent message passed from one generation of alcoholics and addicts to another.

A fellow recovering alcoholic describes his experience in this way:

"When I would grovel and beg my wife not to leave me because of one of my drunken periods, she would take advantage of that. I hated myself and I hated her. I've since come to understand just how much alcoholics hate themselves. The times when I really hated myself the most were those times when I was willing to promise anything because I did not understand that I had a disease. So in sharing my story, I can identify when I'm helping someone and I hear the self-loathing that they have for themselves and they are willing to talk about it. It is very freeing for them and for me.

"At my second AA meeting, I heard people speaking their truth. I heard people speaking out loud about things that I had buried. When I did think about those things, I sure wouldn't let anybody else know that I was thinking that. These people were comfortably talking about the hell they had been in, and I could identify with them and that place of feeling lost. I could see that they no longer were lost. It was even more about the way that they would speak about things that were traumas to me. They would even joke about these things. And it opened me up to the possibility of looking point-blank at what I suspected to be true: That I had been living a lie.

"The most important message conveyed to me at that second AA meeting was a sense of hope. Once I quickly internalized that sense of hope, it was then safe to admit how terrible the disease really was. I no longer had to stay stuck in It. There was a way out. Even more, I discovered that I did not have to do it myself. I knew I couldn't. Now I could admit the whole thing. Then the whole facade crumbled.

"Eventually, after the initial period of seeing all of this, I had to do a lot of picking up of pieces, a lot of growing, and do the work of becoming sober. But I knew where it was going to go. I knew it was going to be okay. I walked up to the guys at the meeting. I was crying. I told them I really wanted what they had. But I also told them that I didn't believe in God. That was no small deal for me since I was a theology major who was teaching theology. I never had admitted that out loud. And the guy who was later to become my sponsor looked at me and said, 'Why don't you stop asking whether you believe in God or not? The real question is, does God believe in you?' In those days, I had a theological base that would not allow me to think that God would have given up on me.

"They also helped me when I told them that if I go home by myself, I was going to drink. Every time I looked at a little kid's toy on the floor, I'd go down. I would drink. So they drove down and sat with me all night. I was touched that anybody would do that for me. And when they showed up, I just cried and danced around the room and it scared the hell out of them.

"I said, 'I'm a lousy husband, father, teacher, provider but I'm gonna be all right, I'm going to be okay.' That was twenty-seven years ago today. My life began that night. Everything else was a dress rehearsal.

"I think that I must have been a pain to be around at that particular time in my life because I was just so tickled that I was home free. I could see with great clarity where I had been, and I knew that I was not there any longer."

The last comment of this fellow recovering alcoholic exemplifies the Fourth Promise of Sobriety, "No matter how far down the scale we have gone, we will see how our experience can benefit others." It is amazing that, no matter what our "bottom" experience was, or how low we sank due to the devastating effects of our addiction to drugs and alcohol, sharing it not only helped us, but miraculously, it helped others. Sharing our journey to this point not only cuts the basic sense of despair and isolation that accompanies our struggle with addiction, but it also affirms and validates the moment-to-moment progress that we have made in our own eyes and in the eyes of others.

Bringing Light to Dark Subjects

The Fourth Promise of Sobriety, "No matter how far down the scale we have gone, we will see how our experience can benefit others," speaks directly to the Fourth Step of Alcoholics Anonymous, "Made a searching and fearless moral inventory of ourselves." Once we have tasted the incremental beginnings of a new happiness and freedom (the First Promise), started utilizing the past to learn how to live better in the present (the Second Promise), and, because of this, began to experience a sense of serenity and peace (the Third Promise), the stage is set for experiencing the Fourth Promise. With all of this groundwork done through working the first three Steps—admitting that we have an illness that we cannot control, opening ourselves up to wisdom that comes from outside of ourselves, and then giving up control to that outside power—we are now ready to look at ourselves and take a moral inventory.

One of the many ways that this process of inventory-taking occurs is by sharing our experience with others. While we may later create a written inventory list, quite often the sharing of our experience is the icebreaker to this most helpful Step. While we are speaking to others about how the disease has affected us, we are bringing light to dark subjects. We are freeing up energy that was previously used for secret-keeping by sharing the secrets of our drinking and using habits.

Try asking yourself the following questions to discover whether the meaning of the Fourth Promise has importance and interest to you:

1. Do I hold on to and purposely not share personal information about myself because I fear abandonment by people who are significant to me?

2. Am I, as an adult, behaving in ways that used to work well to keep me feeling as safe as a child but that today serve no real purpose, such as keeping my thoughts to myself, staying as invisible as possible, or not showing any emotion no matter how strongly I feel it?

3. What do I actually and realistically have to lose by talking about the experiences that led me to this point in my suffering as a result of addiction, either my own or that of someone I care about?

4. What do I actually and realistically have to gain?

5. What can I recall feeling when I have spoken the truth about my circumstances at any time in the past?

6. What actually happened, despite my feelings, when I have spoken the truth about my circumstances at any time in the past?

Once you have answered these questions, review your answers several times at different time periods. If you have detected in your answers a difference between what you wrote and what you thought you should have written, then you may well have been influenced in a positive way by what you have read so far. The Fourth Promise of Sobriety may already be occurring for you.

To review the Fourth Promise of Sobriety:

~The disease of addiction causes us to distance ourselves from others. We need other people for survival.

~The antidote from distancing ourselves from others is to become part of a community or social group.

~The deadly outcome of social disconnection of our ancient past is no different from the real and symbolic soul-death that takes place as a result of this disease.

～Nearly all treatments for addiction share common methods, and nearly all involve a reconnecting with others in a group.

～Sharing our experience benefits us and others in many ways.

～Sharing our experience with others destroys harmful beliefs from childhood and creates new beliefs that involve positive adult actions.

～The Fourth Step of Alcoholics Anonymous is parallel to the Fourth Promise of Sobriety.

PROM #6

CHAPTER FIVE
That Feeling of Uselessness
and Self-Pity Will Disappear

Let's release the past
when sometimes we didn't really know
what or how we wanted to be
so now we're here
when it's great to be the new me.
For I'm now self-loved and self-responsible.
Yes, I am a miracle.
Thank you God!

—A grateful new one

A woman who has been enjoying the Fifth Promise of Sobriety shares her story:

"I had sobered up in springtime, when the air was crisp and cool. It was quiet out, not a lot of noises and quiet inside too. I hadn't had a chance to get my head off and running yet. I remember that I had gotten to my AA meeting early. There were only a couple of cars in the parking lot. I got out of the car and walked over toward the door, trying to figure out whether I really wanted to go inside yet. I found myself staying outside, just looking around. It was then I had A Moment. The kind of moment that I had never experienced before in my life.

"I remember looking into the sky, looking around, feeling the coolness of the air and thinking just how much at peace I was with myself. I was finally at peace with God. I felt that God was beginning to forgive me and that I was beginning to forgive myself. It was very important to know that this was beginning to happen for me. Before this moment, it was all uselessness and self-pity. After this moment, it was peace."

The Fifth Promise of Sobriety speaks to this type of moment.

It says, "That feeling of uselessness and self-pity will disappear."

When the disease of addiction is active in our lives, we feel that we are truly useless. We know the truth of it soon after the disease gets its negative grip on the goodness in our lives. Spending precious energy developing and then chasing around the lies, manipulations, schemes, and the follow-up damage of addiction brings the feeling into reality. We are rendered useless for anything else but more support for the disease.

In the early stages of the disease, we still have the capacity to know that we are less and less effective in acting upon our own internal wisdom and goodness. We begin to feel the loss of these attributes and often show symptoms of grief. We bargain with ourselves to convince ourselves that what we are losing is not really a loss; it is circumstantial, and if only things were different it wouldn't happen again, if only our luck would change, if only this or that had not happened and forced us to take care of our feelings in the only way we knew how.

As our goodness slips away in favor of empowering the disease and Its related behavior, we begin to dislike ourselves. Our lives slowly but surely become pitiful. We build a mask of competence even while we know that it is only a small part of what we used to have before we gave up our integrity and honesty.

A Window of Truth

When the disease progresses further, even the consciousness about the loss of our honesty and integrity begins to flicker and fade along with the usurping of our own goodness. When our health is restored in recovery, we can see how slow this takeover occurred. It can seem as though the loss of our self-esteem, self-confidence, and usefulness slipped away like the slow eroding of a grand mountain. Like lights dimming in indistinguishable increments, our precious attributes fade, become less important, and then disappear entirely. When it happens this slowly, others can barely tell that our souls have been robbed of their light, that the room of our goodness has become dark. And by this trick of the disease, others aren't able to help us. How can they when nobody can see the damage until it is so outrageously hurtful that instead of help, we receive the shunning that we feared most?

Here, another recovering alcoholic speaks:

"My wife left me and was not going to come back until I did something about my drinking. Frequently people coming into AA are in that same place, where their significant other has left them. My initiation into AA brought me to an emotional and spiritual place where I was free of my addiction, but I was also clear that I needed to get sober for myself. That meant being willing to let my wife go. The lights came on for me in a very dramatic way at my second AA meeting. She had been gone and I was filled with self-pity and hopelessness. I had a sense of futility and thought, What's the use?

"It changed when I received a spiritual gift of understanding, or a kind of window of truth. I had a global understanding of everything being done. Not only did I not have to drink any longer, but I realized that my life had been a lie. I realized that I did not have to live that lie.

"I was excited and not bluffing when I called my wife and told her that I was very sorry for what she had had to go through and, as a matter of fact, that she may have to go, that I really would not like that to happen but if we have to get divorced, it's okay and I'm going to be all right. That was a complete about-face from the idea that I couldn't live without her and I couldn't live without alcohol. I realized that I could and would live without both if needed.

"Over the years of my sobriety, so many of the guys I see were in a similar place. They were losing a double addiction whether they realized it or not. What they don't realize is the freedom involved in getting to let go of both their alcohol and their spouses or significant others. And, as a matter of fact, this makes it possible for them to be in relationships with others because it allows them to see that they have a disease and they have to recover from it.

"I have been tremendously grateful for my own personal experience in that turnaround, but it also puts me into a place of empathy and compassion for others so that I can help guide them through that place of self-pity and explain what is involved in the letting go. To help them get to a place where their lives are not being dictated to by either their spouse or their drug."

The disease is good at taking our goodness from us, but even without trying, we attempt to hold on to it because we are naturally good souls. It doesn't leave us without a fight. Here and there the consciousness flickers back on. At times it can be terrifying when we can see for a moment what is really happening to us. And that is when we feel self-pity.

A Gradual Turn for the Better

Here is another story of a woman with twenty-eight years of sobriety. Even given her circumstances, it is clear that sobriety brings an important gift.

"When my husband came home and said that he was having relations with another woman, I was devastated. I took 150 pills, heavy-duty stuff. My attitude at the time was that my children would be better off without me, that I was not a good mother, that I probably was alcoholic and I did not really know what an alcoholic was in those days. I thought that my husband would be better off being free to do what he wanted to do. I left two suicide notes. One was for my husband and one was for my minister. While the minister never read his letter, my husband read his and had the police bring me to a hospital.

"Now all this happened back about thirty years ago when

they didn't know what to do with alcoholics. I was put into a sanitarium where they changed my addiction by giving me tranquilizers. The psychiatrist would come once a week and I would get pills every morning and night. My children were taken from me, my home was invaded, and my possessions taken. My husband took me to court where he tried to get custody of my children once I was discharged from the mental hospital. He was trying to prove that I was crazy in order to win his case.

"One of the things that saved me was, at just the right moment during the worst part of the proceedings, my lawyer reached under the table and grabbed my hand. That gave me enough strength so that I could get through the ordeal.

"I won the case, but lost the battle with alcohol once again shortly thereafter. I drank and missed a lot of work. I worried that I would lose my job. I went to my pharmacist for help. I said, 'Give me something to help me with my drinking.' He gave me the number for Alcoholics Anonymous. I couldn't believe he did that, but I called AA and began going to meetings, being both fascinated as well as scared. I could see that there was something there. Something spiritual, unnamable. I wanted what I saw that those people had at those meetings, but I couldn't figure out what it was.

"I kept hanging around AA, and as the feelings of uselessness and self-pity began to leave me, as I began to feel worthwhile, helpful, and fortunate, I began to get it."

For many with this disease, there came a time when we received the message that we were not enough. Not pretty or handsome enough. Not smart enough. Not athletic enough. Not successful enough. Not talented enough. Being particularly sensitive by nature, many of us did not need to even hear these words. Oftentimes we received this message with looks or through a certain type of negative treatment. But we knew what was meant, and we believed it. More than anything we wanted to be whole. Since nothing we did seemed to get the response that meant "You are enough, just as you are now," we went to great lengths to soothe the hurt feelings and fill up the void inside caused from feeling less worthy than we perceived that others were.

Our drugs of choice often gave temporary relief and sometimes even provided a facade of attractiveness and worthiness. Once we had even so much as a fleeting feeling that we were worth something, we wanted more of the same, again and again. The paradox of addiction is that these experiences are rare, fleeting, and then nonexistent. They are chock-full with glittery excitement but as fulfilling as a meal of tinfoil. The false moments of "enough-ness" and "worthiness" that our chemicals create are like an attractive fishing lure that, once swallowed, turns out to be a dull and deadly piece of lead.

Born Whole and Complete

It is a burden to spend one's life feeling useless and lacking in self-esteem. It is difficult to wake up in the morning and want to participate in what the world has to offer if one feels this way. Of course we know that we didn't ask for this feeling inside. We know that it had to be caused from an outside source. So we feel victimized not only initially by the person who made us feel that we were not enough, but also by the entire world when it reinforces that message in the myriad of ways that it can. The job we did not get, the scholarship that went to someone else, the man or woman of our dreams who left for greener pastures, the errant insult by a frustrated stranger that seemed tailor-made for us—these things re-injure the wound and have us swimming in self-pity very quickly.

We ask, Why does the world pick on me? Why me? Why do others get this or that and not me? What is wrong with me? Why am I never enough?

But the truth is that we were born whole and complete and we never ceased being so. We were always enough, and we still are. Through the belief of others and, later, through chemical dependency, our perception of ourselves changed. Our perception of ourselves became one of diminishing returns, of negativity, of saving face, of wearing a mask, of feeling fake, of being found out, of loss of self-esteem. The list is unfortunately endless. But we were real all the time. Through the lens of addictive disease, we just could not see it.

One of the delightful and frequent gifts of sobriety is a renewal of our self-esteem and a dropping of the feeling of uselessness and self-pity. The solitary act of not picking up a drink or a drug is a major contributor to this quick perception improvement. We soon find there are positive things that we can do instead of so many things that we cannot do. The operative word here is *do.*

Action, or becoming useful, is the antidote to feelings of uselessness and self-pity. Basic sobriety brings with it the ability to see how harmful procrastination can be, and a program of recovery that includes taking action on the things we can change (as opposed to giving up due to all of the things that we cannot change) brings the gift of the Fifth Promise to us.

On a microscopic biological level, we are no longer stripping our brain cells of what they need to reach a state of chemical balance. These cells struggle to heal and rebalance. Even a minute improvement on the neurochemical level can be felt in the body and in the mood on a global level. Whether or not alcoholics/addicts can see this happen in themselves, others tend to see this change quickly. Often this change is pivotal in bringing back a positive support system, often long before the chemically dependent person believes he or she is worthy of such help and support.

The growth process is attractive to other people, despite injuries that we may have imposed upon them during our active using phase. The energy we used to spend on mood regulation is now spent on many valuable things, and the outcome of this positive energy expenditure is the rudimentary beginnings of nonmedicated, wholly genuine self-esteem.

On a macrocosmic level, the restoration of circadian rhythms, the rebalancing of daily habits, the return to work, the restoration of assets lost, friendships regained, family reunited has a tremendous effect on the newly recovering person's sense of self-worth. Beyond the biological level are other areas that tend to go along for the ride. Because this disease attacks Its victim on the biological, psychological, and social levels, It easily stays camouflaged unless all of these areas are addressed in recovery.

A Change in Priorities

Treatment programs usually address these three areas in an effort to promote long-term sobriety. In a traditional thirty-day treatment program, the promise of having that sense of uselessness and self-pity leave us is often fulfilled before one even has a chance to successfully discharge from the program.

Psychologically, where our drinking or drug use has caused its own brand of depression, the simple passage of clean and sober time improves our mood, which helps us become honest, open, and willing to try new things. A brain that is saturated in solvent (i.e., alcohol) is hell-bent on self-preservation and avoiding discomfort, not learning new social skills. The thrill that might have come from obtaining, bargaining, hiding, and lying about drugs or alcohol is now found in the challenge of speaking about oneself in a group and of connecting with other people, often for the first time. The priorities turn from the life-zapping struggle to preserve the using environment to the challenge and pleasure involved in the development of a clean and sober environment. Social connections are either learned for the first time or relearned in a healthier way without benefit of the smoothing out or socially "lubricating" effect of mood-altering substances.

Some people liken this experience to what it must be like to walk on the moon or to be an infant walking upright for the very first time. It feels so breathtakingly odd to realize that we are enough, just as we are, without embellishment, without our false mask of competence, and without our periodic doses of chemical confidence. It is thrilling to learn, through recovery, that we came into this world with built-in gifts and that with time and healing, we can have these gifts restored and available to us.

Working a good program means adding one more area to the list of places within ourselves that require repair, and that area is called spirituality. The disease of addiction, along with damaging our ability to see ourselves accurately and to make a strong, heartfelt connection with others, also disconnects us from a meaningful relationship with our Higher Power, however we choose to perceive that spiritual concept.

This idea of a power greater than ourselves is fundamental to the idea of an effective recovery program and is the singular most important difference between merely quitting the use of a substance and gaining a meaningful, worthwhile, fulfilling life as a result of sobriety.

One recovering man describes his sobriety in this way:

"In sobriety, many new things in life are available. Like freedom. After accepting that I'm an alcoholic and surrendering to the process of that disease, and continually accepting and reaccepting it to prevent any attitude of denial from slipping in, I feel free from the consequences. That is one of the reasons that I go to AA meetings. Sometimes it is simply to say, 'Hi, I'm Robert and I'm an alcoholic.' To act on the denial at the outset is to be able to easily say that phrase with acceptance of it. And it's okay to say that I'm an alcoholic because I used to be a drunk. Today I'm a sober alcoholic and that's a big, big difference. That's one of the rewards of sobriety. Freedom from this chemical dependence.

"The spirituality, the fellowship, and the support of the AA program are so important. When I went to treatment, I finally decided that I couldn't get sober alone. I tried. So during the treatment process, I got sober. After that I went to AA and stayed sober with a support program. It isn't good to be alone, and we don't want to be alone. Through this process I learned the importance of the saying, 'no pain, no gain.' As I went along I learned that my pain was a stepping stone to my recovery and my recovery was my life. So my pain gave me my life. When I can accept my adversity, I can have a better life.

"Recently, I've been thinking about the importance of self-worth. Self-worth is not self-importance. There is a big difference. Self-importance for me is deciding that I can do it alone, deciding that I need to feed my ego, and ego is important but not to the point that it takes over my humility.

"Blending my feelings with my thinking is another gift that I get through my recovery. It is important that these two are in balance throughout the day. Also in my sober life it is important that I feel gratitude. Gratitude is tied up with my spirituality. Just like the end of chapter 5 in the Big Book, with the ABCs. *A* is that we were alcoholic and could not manage our own lives. *B* is that no human power could have relieved our alcoholism. *C* is that God could and would if he were sought. I think that it is important for me to transfer my dependence on alcohol to that of spirituality in order to supersede my addiction. The Promises of Sobriety talk about God doing for us what we could not do for ourselves, and that is one of the Promises that I must rely on for myself. It has to do with my spirituality. It supports my sobriety and keeps my ego trimmed back. Because the *ism* in alcoholism stands for *I, self,* and *me.* I don't want to forget it. I don't need the ego.

"One needs some sense of ego, I suppose, to support a level of self-esteem. I didn't have that when I was drinking. I had a big masquerade instead. I have to blend my ego with humility. If I do, I won't be egotistical or, worse, I won't be arrogant. I don't seek applause. I've had a lot of accomplishments but don't need recognition. That's just the way I am. For recovery, that works well. I've heard people say, 'I need to be needed.' I don't feel that way. I don't need a reward to be of service to someone.

"The AA medallion that I carry on my key chain is a regular reminder that I must be honest with myself. Every time I go to start my car, it reminds me of what it says, 'To thine own self be true.' This is another part of my support thought process. I was a hospice volunteer for eight years, until I experienced some burnout, then I stopped. But before I burned out, I felt gratitude every day. If you help out someone who is dying and you don't feel gratitude, something's really wrong! It wasn't self-gratification so much as it was an open gratification for life as it is, not life as I wished it would be. That kind of service work was very humbling but also had a positive effect on my sobriety. It teaches me that I don't have the authority to be a judge. It shows me that I'm not in control. It keeps any sense of self-pity I might have from overcoming me.

"One of the gifts of my sobriety includes being able to think about and identify what the purpose in my life is all about. And secondly, what are my priorities? It is just as important that I have a purpose in life as it is for a company to have a mission statement. Every six months I look these two ideas over and make adjustments as needed. I may need to change priorities. But it keeps me grounded in having the right attitude about everything: gratitude.

"When I went through treatment, it was supposed to be twenty-eight days. Just before the final weekend, I decided that I felt great. I felt confident that I would be okay. So I figured if I was feeling this good, I should be able to leave treatment early so I could get back to work first thing Monday morning. My counselor saw right through my confidence and said, 'The staff met this morning and talked all about your case, especially since you are getting ready to leave next week. We all concluded that you are too damn cocky.' So I thought, okay then, I'll just leave on my original date.

"Then my counselor said, 'Since you are so cocky, and so ready to leave, we know that just the opposite is true. You are in danger if you leave now. Therefore, we don't want you to leave next Wednesday; we want you to leave a week from next Wednesday. You need it!' He told me that it was a good investment, this extra one week out of my entire life, if only it could make a better foundation for my future sobriety. I got up and said, 'End of discussion. I'll stay.'

"I knew they were right. And their truth humbled me. It has been that very humility that has given me all the gifts of sobriety that I now have. Thirteen years of gifts. Now I am sober. Now I have a new sense of self-worth. Now I am honest with myself and others. It was the taking action in standing up and giving over blind faith to them that kept me feeling victimized by my own program. I had learned how to keep self-pity at bay just by taking that one simple action. Contentment, self-worth, self-esteem, peace within, acceptance, gratitude, these are all gifts of my sobriety. The gift of usefulness and loss of self-pity has been major."

Misery Becomes Optional

To follow the earlier premise that the Fifth Step of AA, "Admitted to God, to ourselves, and to another human being the exact nature of our wrongs," parallels the Fifth Promise is to acknowledge that sobriety gives us an opportunity to finally replace our self-pity with constructive action. Admitting wrongs is taking strong action and moving out of the victim role.

One of the many gifts of sobriety is that misery becomes optional. Taking action is exactly what we are able to do once sobriety has been established. The disease protects itself by lying in self-pity and procrastination in everything that we do. It is easy to see through another story of action in recovery, below, that usefulness is a gift of sobriety that keeps on giving . . . both to the giver and the recipient.

"I used to be steeped in uselessness and self-pity. I don't know if it was a chicken or egg thing, in that I felt useless and pitied myself, therefore I numbed that feeling out with drugs, or if numbing myself out with drugs made me feel useless and so I felt a lot of self-pity. Either way you look at it, it stunk. However, this is not the case any longer. I had felt useless because, truthfully, I was not using myself to do anything for myself or the world that was productive or based in kindness or other-centeredness. Everything I did for myself or the world was so that things would come back to me, and the sooner the better. The program talks about being selfish in a healthy way. . . . Well back when I was using, I was not at all healthily selfish. I was just self-centered, and this is what fired the feelings of uselessness and self-pity."

To review the Fifth Promise of Sobriety:
~The disease of addiction usurps our own sense of goodness, replacing it with a false and negative concept of ourselves.
~Sobriety immediately begins to restore our ability to take action.
~Drugs and alcohol rob us of the sense that "we are enough," or that we are just fine as we are, unmedicated. This results in a loss of a sense of usefulness as well as a loss of self-esteem.
~Action is the antidote to feelings of uselessness and self-pity.
~Spiritual connection keeps the sense of self in relative proportion to the world as it is, and a balanced sense of self has no need for self-pity.

~The Fifth Step of AA relates to the Fifth Promise of Sobriety because taking strong action moves us out of the uselessness of the victim role and bolsters self-esteem.

PROM #7

CHAPTER SIX

We Will Lose Interest in Selfish Things
and Gain Interest in Our Fellows

I am a good, kind, giving person. The gift of my sobriety is that for today, I can reach beyond my protective wall and connect with others meaningfully. I feel worthy of knowing about others and of being known. I am now able to see and appreciate my own goodness because I see it reflected in the goodness of others.

If we feel that we are not worthy of being known, we act out that unworthiness with others. The worldview that accompanies addiction is a negative one. We suspect that we have this problem, but we also mistakenly suspect that we inherited a defective personality. We often feel as though we are naturally negative, naturally "bad," naturally cynical, and, most of all, naturally selfish. But this is not true, even if we have been told that it is so by those we respect, such as parents or other authority figures.

Because we carry the marker for addictive disease, we may very well be more sensitive by nature. We more easily take on these negative projections by those we care about as we grow up. We may also make good movie projection screens for self-image problems that really belong to other people. Youngsters who grow up in such an environment don't see what's going on and believe most everything that older people tell them. Therefore, as adults we often hold beliefs about ourselves that have nothing to do with who we really are. Nonetheless, we believe we have defects in our character, whether we came to this conclusion by ourselves or through the assistance of someone we respected or looked up to.

Part of making a decision to enter recovery and claim this Sixth Promise of Sobriety is being willing to give up these so-called defects of character. The Sixth Step of Alcoholics Anonymous states, "Were entirely ready to have God remove all these defects of character." This Step parallels the Sixth Promise of Sobriety. If we have opened up our eyes and hearts to the possibility that we are innately good, kind, loving, giving people at our core—and that it is the *disease* that insists upon a belief system of badness, unkindness, and selfishness to maintain itself—we have gone a long way in realizing the Sixth Promise.

With a clear mind, healthier body, and opened heart, we are able to hear and see the struggles of others. It not only becomes a part of our recovery program to help those who still suffer from the disease of addiction, but it also becomes part of our very belief system that such behavior is natural for us. "Bad" people do not help others. "Good" people do. As time goes on, we become part of an ever growing family of "good people." This makes us attractive to others and easy to be around, as well as raises our self-esteem and sense of self-worth. As we continue to gain time in sobriety and get to know this new, positive part of ourselves better, our body, mind, and spirit are becoming used to the new way of existing. Slowly our old concepts of ourselves slip away.

Global and Radical Changes

It is said by many holistic and Eastern health practitioners that over a period of several years, every single cell of our body is replaced by a brand-new cell. They write that if we are willing to take action to make changes, even our cells go along with these changes and the new cells tell an entirely different story about what we are made of. Perhaps this is why you can look at recovering men or women of one year and see that they look better and certainly feel better about themselves. But when you look at people with seven or more years of recovery, you see more global and radical changes. It is as if they have been given a new set of insides and, often, outsides. Of course, addictive disease is not caught early enough in far too many instances and has already done irreparable damage. But, even so, the profound changes that recovery brings to those who suffer damage are obviously well worth the trouble to get and stay sober.

For many of us, it is difficult to figure this particular Promise out because it seems to require such a huge adjustment in one's picture of oneself. But the reality is that our self-perception shifts over time, in such small increments that we can barely see ourselves changing until most of the change has taken place. Many people in recovery don't believe that the Sixth Promise has come true until years' worth of evidence has accumulated. That is how cunning, baffling, and powerful the disease of addiction is. Even when we have a major gift of sobriety in our very possession, we may miss the joy of owning it.

Gradually, with moment-to-moment sobriety, our thoughts turn from inward spinning about how to stay safe, how to cover our tracks and lies, how to maintain a supply of our drink or drug, to outward thoughts, focused on others. Much of our time is freed up and we develop new habits that support using that time wisely. Once the first several Promises begin to come true, many of us find ourselves willing to do what we would never have considered before: give unselfishly of ourselves and our time.

No Longer Self-Centered

Here is a brief account by a woman who finds her self-worth through her acts of great humanity and compassion toward others. This is a woman who once believed that she was hateful, naturally selfish, and self-centered. She said that her drinking was chaotic because it was so complex: She drank in spite of negative self-beliefs, because of it as well as to serve it and to make such ugliness as true as possible. She drank just to drink, forgetting to have a good reason at times. She then noted, with a smile, that it is so much easier to enjoy the gift of her sobriety because of its simplicity: The one thing she still understands that is so very precious, the one single reason to stay sober at times, is that her sobriety gives her a magnificent feeling of self-lessness, even more than alcohol could.

"I am with the AIDS Project. I go into the homes of those who are sick with that disease and clean for them. Trust me when I say that I'm not domestic, but what are these people supposed to do? They don't have the money or the energy. They simply can't clean up for themselves. Two nights each week I work on the HIV ward at the local hospital. Here is why: In 1987, a friend of mine got AIDS. He did not tell me. One day when he greeted me, he didn't give me a kiss. That was very uncharacteristic of him, as usually, being quite flamboyant in general, he would grab me when we'd first meet, throw me back and kiss me, and scream out, 'Kiss me you perverted female!' We'd laugh just at that alone until tears came. I knew something was wrong when he wouldn't kiss me hello anymore. It was on that day that he told me his kidney had been acting up. I said, 'You've lost weight too. Let me stuff you full of Mexican food and you'll be happy.'

"He declined and gave me a 'Hollywood hug' as we parted, meaning that we hugged with absolutely no human connection whatsoever. Turns out that two days later, he had left town because he was embarrassed and ashamed. He went to his parents' home in his parents' state where he was not accepted and wanted. He probably had to lie about his disease and his entire life's contents to them. And then he died with people around him who did not love him at all, much less love him for just who he was. That is when I said, 'Never again. I don't care what I have to do, but nobody that I care for will ever die alone, unloved, again.'

"Despite the fact that my entire family frowns on what I do in my service work, I know that it is right in my heart. My sane, sober brain and whole spirit tells me so, and because I know how I used to be—closed off and self-centered, selfish and loaded with self-pity—I know that what I do is absolutely right. I can follow my heart because I can know my heart now. Knowing what my heart says is the same thing as knowing what God says. My sobriety lets me listen and allows me to act unselfishly toward others. When I was drunk, I couldn't hear my heart, couldn't follow its message, and never had the feeling that I was anything but good for nothing."

In this story, the recovering alcoholic realized, thanks to her sobriety, that her own belief systems, taken on from messages by others, did not work well for her. In sobriety, she was able to see clearly that acting out of self-lessness and kindness toward others, any others in need, was the right thing to do despite her family's negative belief systems. She heard the voice of her own heart and intuitively knew this was a higher voice, even though the concept of God baffled her. We will get to more about the concept of a Higher Power in the final two chapters of this book.

Stop Feeding the Disease

Beliefs about ourselves that do not work well for us, that keep us in a cycle of self-hatred and disconnectedness from others, must be given up. For many, giving up our belief and supporting actions of being selfish is frightening. What will we do once we stop behaving selfishly and become more outwardly focused, gaining "interest in our fellows"? If we aren't selfish, then what *are we*? The fear of having nothing to replace our old belief is enough to keep us participating in the cycle of addiction indefinitely.

We are not selfish by nature. We are not bad people with serious character flaws. If suddenly our disease were to be entirely removed from us, the need to be inwardly focused would disappear. Remember chapter 3's comparison of the disease of addiction to a petri dish that needs a fresh supply of nutrients in order to keep growing itself. If we were able to hold on to some level of self-esteem, if we had positive beliefs about ourselves that were durable enough to withstand the opinions and prejudices of others, the petri dish would quickly dry up. The disease would have nothing negative to feed upon.

The disease of addiction quickly thrives on negativity and slowly dies in a positive environment.

The disease of addiction also uses our best talents and natural gifts to preserve Itself. Let's say that you are a wonderful salesperson. All of the interpersonal gifts that you would normally harness to make incredible sales would slowly and surely be utilized by the disease. The good news is that you can begin reclaiming the positive gifts you forfeited to support the disease as soon as you enter recovery.

As soon as your brain begins to heal (the healing process begins fairly quickly for most people, once the substance is entirely removed), you gain the ability to change your perception about yourself and others. In a way, it is as if the mouth closes (the part of us that speaks so that we do not have to listen) and the ears open (the part of us that is willing to take in new information and act upon it).

Being an active alcoholic or addict involves living with a self-perpetuating cycle of negativity. The disease of addiction causes us to be ever vigilant, protective of our secrets, selective of our confidants, excluding of family and well-meaning reformers. If It does not succeed in keeping away connection with others, It puts Itself in jeopardy of being found out, discovered, and annihilated. The desperation we feel to have "just one more" reflects the desperation of the disease to hang on to us so that It can thrive.

Some of us do not have a sense of desperation. Instead, we have, in between our binges, a huge attitude of false overconfidence. We tell ourselves that just because we don't drink in the morning or use drugs alone, just because we groom ourselves well and don't resemble the stereotypical drunk or addict living in the streets, we cannot possibly be alcoholics or addicts. The size of this overconfidence is yet another reflection of how much energy the disease requires to hide Itself.

Relationships Increase in Value

People in recovery receive one of the great gifts of sobriety when they realize that, without embellishment, they lack nothing to find serenity, peace, and happiness. When a person's full potential is no longer wrapped up in supporting the disease, it is free to attune itself to positive rewards. Since recovery involves developing a strong connection with a power greater than oneself, and because this connection erases the emptiness that was once felt inside, the recovering person begins to value material things less and spiritual and interpersonal relationships more. A recovering man talks about his experience with this:

"There have been so many outstanding incidents in my life. When I was working in a halfway house, I met a guy who was a heroin addict. He had been places that I couldn't even think about going to. I characterize myself as a 'high-bottom drunk' compared to where heroin had taken this guy. He called me up one night at about three o'clock in the morning. He didn't want to live anymore. I got him to a hospital right away, where he detoxed.

"He is now six years clean and sober. His life has blossomed. Entirely changed. Not only is he better at what he does for a living, but he is healthier to other people because of his own recovery. That is a miracle, because this guy was spiritually dead for sure. There are other guys like him. They grow and change, then call me up and try to pat me on the back. They say, 'Thank you, I owe you my life.' But the truth is that I'm so grateful to have known them, to have been associated with them at all. I was just there at the right time, when I was placed there by my Higher Power. I didn't do a thing. I can't take credit for miracles."

When, through recovery, the definitions of *gain, wealth,* and *plenty* change, many addicts and alcoholics discover that they have all they need to be happy in the here and now. This is because the disease of addiction is past or future based and the recovery process involves focusing on the here and now. In this very moment, it is possible to be satiated and full. But to anticipate what will happen in the next moment is to desire fullness or satisfaction, and it is this very desire that begins the repetitive insanity of addiction.

Living in this moment is dangerous to the persona of addiction. It does not want us to be focused on our pleasure in this moment. It wants us to feel shame and regret for the past and anxiety and stress over the future. It breeds and multiplies best when we are not in the moment. A person who has no outward, false desires cannot be tempted to relapse back to addiction. Once relieved of the burden of having to repeat addiction's insane thought process, people are free to focus on themselves, make behavior changes, stay out of the past and the future, and, in so doing, experience the riches that every blessed moment on this earth, in this form, brings.

To review the Sixth Promise of Sobriety:
~People who are addicted to drugs or alcohol often believe that they are naturally "bad" and carry this so-called character defect as if it is a birthright.
~The Sixth Promise of Sobriety answers the Sixth Step of AA in that we give up these character defects and thereafter begin to experience our own works of goodness as they are reflected in the lives of others.
~As we progress in our healing time, our thoughts turn from ourselves to others and our definition of ourselves continues to progress in a positive manner.

～The clarity that sobriety brings opens up our hearts so that we can make better independent judgments about what we will choose to do, how we will behave, and how, as a result, we will regard ourselves.

～The disease uses our best talents and skills to support Itself, therefore It attempts to keep us from discovering our goodness.

～Living in each moment instead of past or future moments allows us to view ourselves more accurately.

CHAPTER SEVEN
Self-Seeking Will Slip Away

Today I will enjoy the Seventh Promise by giving up my desire to serve the needs of addiction. I will make a conscious choice as many times as it takes in this day to question everything I think is best, knowing that the disease would have me thinking that I, not another, knows what is best for me. I will stop feeding addictive behaviors with isolation and with feeling one-down or one-up. I will begin seeking ways to connect with others on any level possible. I know if I do this that gradually my habit of manipulating people, places, and things to get them just how I want them will slip away.

If the disease of addiction is about anything, it is about changing our need to control people, places, and things. In order to stop the progression of the disease, a major change of one's attitude about life is necessary. Nothing new can happen if all of the old beliefs that held the disease in place are still operational.

The gift resulting from changing our attitude is that we are able to be more relaxed, more accepting, less prone to negative symptoms that arise from stress. We learn to be flexible, to see the gray area rather than the absolutes of situations. The Seventh Promise, "Self-seeking will slip away," begins to come true as soon as we make behavior and attitude changes.

The disease of addiction requires an incredible amount of control. Due to the disease, the practicing alcoholic/addict is self-centered. Situations must be controlled in order to manipulate people, places, and things into a direct delivery system where the terminus, or end point, is ourselves. The disease causes us not to care whether this system is fair or whether It shares the resources we bring to ourselves. It only cares to preserve Itself. The disease causes us to be selfish in an unhealthy way, self-seeking and narcissistic. We would not be able to pre-serve the disease if It would allow us to care about the conse-quences of our actions to ourselves and others.

It is easy to picture what happens as the disease of addiction progresses if you imagine a constricting circle that begins around the soul of the addict or alcoholic and grows outside the body, looking more and more like a bull's-eye as it expands. This bull's-eye pulls many things into its targeted center and keeps them in. Nothing escapes it.

Some of the things that get pulled into the center of this closed circle, and often used up or destroyed, are other people's money, living quarters, food, bail, jobs (or favors to avoid the loss of a job), relationships, integrity, trust . . . the list can be endless once the vortex begins. As the addiction gets fed in this manner, self-seeking grows stronger.

Controlling people, places, and things requires vigilance and extreme attentiveness to detail. A tension in the spirit, in the lifestyle, in the body, in any relationships begins to develop and spread. Controlling, self-seeking behavior causes a withholding of one's resources, as well. Resources are not always monetary. In this case, one's resources might be the ability to be affection-ate or to care about things that hold no direct personal benefit. It is not unusual to hear a child of an addicted parent complain in verbal and physical ways of such a lack of attention or affec-tion. Marriages have failed because of this self-seeking mode of addiction: It sends energy *in* to the addict/alcoholic, instead of sending energy *out* toward others, toward community.

A True Sense of Relaxation

Recovery brings with it the ability to gradually grow or regrow trust in oneself and in others. This trust causes a reversal in the energy distribution of a recovering person, from self-seeking to other-giving. Not being on guard, not dealing with being found out, not having paranoia, finally getting rested and fed and connected with all serves to reverse the energy flow of the disease. Feeling relaxed, the disease cannot grow. It is difficult to stay in a relaxed state and think up lies and schemes at the same time. A trusting, relaxed state of being, which is sometimes quickly and sometimes slowly brought about through the recovery process, is the enemy of the disease. The two states do not coexist. The disease can create a false sense of relaxation, but this is temporary and, once again, controlled via a mood-altering substance. Only a real, recovery-induced relaxation can keep this disease at bay.

Recovery allows one to relax. It cannot be healthy to constantly be on guard, watching for any circumstance that can be played to our best advantage, or, worse, watching for any circumstance that another may be controlling. The change in attitude from rigid to relaxed, from controlling to accepting, from black-and-white to gray, is a positive change, and once this type of change has begun it gains a momentum and movement that leads toward increasing health. The gift of a change in attitude is mental and physical health, which is the antithesis of the disease Itself.

Here is a story of a man with many years of recovery that illustrates how the direction of energy changes once self-seeking behaviors stop.

"Back about twenty years ago, I got a DUI [driving under the influence]. I had been in a blackout for about three days, the officer had pulled me over, ordered me out of the car. I only have just this one or two minutes' recollection of what happened that day. The officer later said that he heard me say something like, 'Why don't you go arrest a *real* criminal?' It was the first time I heard an officer say, 'Mister, you *are* a real criminal. You're no different than a guy who puts a gun to someone's face at the local convenience store.'

"I had never thought of myself as a criminal before, but very soon I began to see that I was. This one or two minutes in time that I can recall seems so fresh in my mind that it feels like it happened no more than fifteen minutes ago. As long as I keep this experience close to me, my attitude is forever changed. This was when the compulsion to drink alcohol was removed for me. As long as I do not forget, as long as I do not become complacent or take this transformative experience for granted, I won't be deceived, I will not have to repeat the past. I will remain changed in a positive way each day for the rest of my life."

A Moment of Clarity

So how do we get this energy to reverse direction from self-seeking to other-giving? For some, it takes many years to achieve. For others, as with the fellow who shares the next story, the about-face happened in a matter of moments, when he had what is commonly called in AA "a moment of clarity."

"Bill Wilson, cofounder of Alcoholics Anonymous, and I became very friendly. He and I had the same kind of recovery. He called it the 'hot flash recovery.' Most people don't recover that way. Read appendix 2 at the end of the Big Book about the educational variety and how you go through some struggles as did Dr. Bob, the other fellow of AA. In other words, sobriety came to me and Bill and a few others . . . on a golden platter! Without even asking for it. The important thing is that it happened, like any attitudinal change, after a moment of intense stress. Intense depression, I can't emphasize this enough, has always preceded emotional change."

Here are two tales from yet another recovering person. The first is about someone who went from self-seeking to other-giving in almost too big of a way:

"There was a guy who was pretty wealthy. He lived in San Francisco. He got sober in AA. So, like many, his altruism was sticking out by about a yard. He decided that since he owned a building downtown, he would configure this building to help drunks. It would sort of be like a treatment center. He had plans to do one sort of thing on the first floor, another on the second floor. Third floor was detox, fourth floor was private counseling. You know, this was all on a very grandiose scale. He then makes up a list of sixty-one rules and he sends them back to New York for Bill Wilson's approval. Bill sent them right back to him and said, 'Add rule number sixty-two.' The guy writes back, 'What is rule number sixty-two?' And the reply said: 'Rule #62: Don't take yourself so damn seriously.'" The second tale is about one who quickly made the transition from self-seeking to other-giving:

"There is a man who lives in the desert. He is nearly fifty years sober and I just love him. One time he said to me, 'When you're having a general conversation and you meet somebody and it starts out like, Hey how's the world treatin' ya? Well that's an opening for a self-centered fool, huh?'

"One night it hit me like a thunderbolt when he greeted me again, but this time he said, 'So, how are you treatin' the world?' That is when I had a major change in attitude. How am I treating the world? What a concept for someone who drank because of how the world treated him!"

My Way or the Highway

It isn't unusual to hear the phrase "I want what I want when I want it" used to describe self-seeking behavior or attitudes that grow stronger with the progression of the addiction. Another phrase common to the recovery community is "My way or the highway." These phrases, or sayings, help us identify the part of the disease that the Seventh Promise addresses.

Tunnel vision is a shortcoming borne of the disease. Where we would never be as narrowly focused before the progression of chemical dependence, now it is nearly impossible not to be. Our way has to be the right way. After all, if we aren't right, then possibly someone else is, and then we just might receive assistance that would break the cycle of the disease. The disease wants to preserve Itself, so there are seldom any moments of clarity where anything other than self-seeking behavior can be exercised.

Step Seven states: "Humbly asked Him to remove our shortcomings." One of our shortcomings has to do with this "my way or the highway" type of behavior. If we aren't busy practicing it while active in our disease, we are busy feeling bad about ourselves as a result of it. Self-seeking behavior is so much a part of the addictive cycle that often it takes an act of a Higher Power to interrupt its movement. Step Seven is the marker along the path to recovery. Once this Step is practiced, we understand that the disease promotes this poor behavior, not the true sense of ourselves. We don't have to feel rotten any longer.

The very act of asking God to remove this shortcoming interrupts the self-seeking cycle, for isn't reaching beyond the authority of ourselves attempting to make connection with another? Isn't this very act the exact opposite of self-seeking behavior? We don't want to stop self-seeking for ourselves; we want to stop this behavior because it hurts those around us. We can't bear their suffering because of our addiction. We can't bear our guilt because of our addiction. Furthermore, Step Seven offers us relief, and Promise Seven, "Self-seeking will slip away," is our reward.

One longtime recovering person describes this Promise in the following way:

"There are still times that I want to do it my way, but I remember how my way got me to where I was. On a daily basis, twenty-four hours a day, before I make a decision, I give it to God as to which way I should really go with it. When I get up in the morning, I say, 'Okay, God, whatever happens, I know there is a purpose for it.' For example, if somebody crosses me during the day, instead of building a resentment over it, I say to myself and to God, 'Okay, what am I supposed to learn out of this experience today?' I give God my day and I know that I'm going to learn something. Whether it be just acceptance or looking at life on life's terms. Most things are not about me, but about others, and I need to get out of the way and let others have their own growth."

The Privilege of Serving Others

Others have more to say about their understanding of the Seventh Promise of Sobriety:

"Grandiosity is my major character defect. I ask God to remove this one outstanding, overriding character defect of mine on a daily basis, and the miracle is, I can now see past my own nose and be selfless. With sobriety, I realize the Seventh Promise when I can get outside of myself and understand that God has made others besides me who are worthy of love, care, and attention.

"With my brain and body free of drugs and alcohol, I can think outwardly rather than inwardly. I am not consumed with finding ways to get my habit served. Rather, I am finding ways to serve others; I know now that this is why I am here on earth. There are a million minute ways to provide service. Opportunities are presented to me each and every day, whether it is to pull over and help someone who has a flat tire, or if I get a call from someone's relative asking for help because they are strung out and want to have what they see me having every day.

"Focusing myself outward and praying to God every morning to show me opportunities to serve the world provide me with a sense of purpose and usefulness that I never had before. A lot of my sense of self-worth and self-esteem comes from just this one thing, actually. I no longer ask God to give things to me or to bring certain experiences my way. I ask God to bring me to places where I am needed, to open my eyes so that I can see the subtlest of areas where I might be of some kind of service. I never know what that will turn out to be, but each day I wake up and this thought excites me. It makes life a complete adventure on a minute-to-minute basis. Where is the time to pity myself when my life is so rich with positive experiences?"

To review the Seventh Promise of Sobriety:
~The Seventh Promise begins to happen as soon as behavior and attitude changes take place.
~Self-seeking behavior occurs as a result of the progression of the disease.
~The control that must be exerted to maintain self-seeking behavior causes a great deal of tension and stress. This tension and stress supports the cycle of addiction as we seek to control It with further drinking or using.
~Recovery reverses the negative energy from self-seeking to other-giving.
~Recovery is relaxing and a stress and tension reducer, promoting the cycle of health.
~The Seventh Step addresses the Seventh Promise in that it often takes intervention in the form of spiritual reconnection and awakening to begin the process of reversing self-seeking behavior.

CHAPTER EIGHT
Our Whole Attitude and Outlook
upon Life Will Change

Today I will be willing to take in new information as it comes to me. I will consider it seriously first, before automatically rejecting it. In this way, I will begin to effect change in my life. I will enjoy the slow but sure evolution of my attitude from negative to positive, letting go of the need to take myself too seriously in this process. I am willing to see irony and humor in areas of life that had not occurred to me before. I am willing to admit to myself that my perception of the world, above most other things, has had a powerful effect on my everyday experience of life. As my perception changes, so will my experience of the world. I will delight in my newfound ability to enjoy this most powerful gift.

The Eighth Step of AA states, "Made a list of all persons we had harmed, and became willing to make amends to them all." The Eighth Promise of Sobriety states, "Our whole attitude and outlook upon life will change." As discussed in earlier chapters, the Twelve Steps of Alcoholics Anonymous can be viewed as markers along a path and each of the Twelve Promises can be viewed as destinations. If we do the tasks suggested in the Steps, we are promised to arrive at very specific destinations.

In the Eighth Step and Eighth Promise, the path points toward being willing to look at ourselves and our actions in great detail. If we are, in fact, willing to do this, we cannot help but make a tremendous transition. That transition is one so pivotal to becoming a self-actualized, happy human being that it is no wonder it took seven difficult Steps to prepare for it.

This is a Step of self-awareness and contemplated action. In the Eighth Step we leave behind our state of being self-focused and become other-focused in a healthy way; this shift enhances rather than detracts from our selves. That is why it is such a tremendous transition. The proverbial back of the disease is broken so that our energy makes a significant change toward health when we work this particular Step.

Using the strengths gained from working through Steps One through Seven, we look into the past and, instead of regretting it, we are able to learn from it. Learning from our past behavior breaks the cycle of insanity caused by addiction. We are now open to learn new behaviors. We are ready to enjoy the gifts that life has to bring us because of attitudinal change.

Our whole attitude and outlook on life changes because we are clearheaded, we have our own inborn wisdom to rely upon, or we can begin to develop this if it is not already there. We are not listening to the disease and Its crazy logic of self-seeking for Its own sake. Our attitude is free to grow and shift from being fear-based to freedom-based. One of the best and most important Promises may be the Eighth Promise, because once our attitude and outlook on life shifts, our perception shifts with it, and this gives us the opportunity to move from our negative position to a positive one. There are very few alcoholics and addicts who aren't aware at some time in their recovery that, because of their negative outlook, they have spent a lot of time waiting for the other shoe to drop when things have been going along just fine.

The Problem with Willpower

It would also be typical of us as addicts and alcoholics to expect that attitude change should happen because we merely want it to. What a setup for failure! When we so will ourselves to change and find that there are little or no results, we revel in our despair and feel tempted to drink or use to relieve those awful feelings of helplessness.

Many of us who have more than a few years of sobriety recall how we had to change certain beliefs that we once thought were permanent and unquestionable. One of these beliefs is that one needs to have something called willpower in order to succeed in life. Those of us who somehow are unable to use this thing called willpower feel shunned, less-than, and defective in our character.

Part of changing our perception involves being willing to look at the belief systems that we bring to the table each and every day, and hold them up to the light. These belief systems need periodic scrutinizing. However threatening to ourselves, others, and even institutions, we need to ask, "Is this belief system working for me?" "Is it promoting my optimal health and well-being?" If the answer is marginal or no, then at this point, it is not willpower that is required, but courage, commitment, and a strong desire to change, for it is the belief system itself, not the person carrying it, that is the problem.

Recently a friend of mine and I were having coffee. We clinked our coffee mugs together in a mock-toast. Then she took a sip. I decided not to and placed my mug on the table. She said, "Hey, that's a tradition! You're supposed to sip after you clink." I thought about this and decided that I did not need a sip after my clink, that the clink of connection was like a wink of recognition and agreement between us, and that this was enough. It was up to me to clink, sip, or opt to do none of the above. In a very small way, this is a good way to describe one of the best parts about being sober. I can make these choices. I realize that this is my world. I'm responsible for carrying on certain traditions or not, depending on my own conscious awareness and agreement. I'm a slave to nothing automatic unless I agree to that too. If you are still addicted to a substance, can you say the same? Although the clinking without sipping tradition is such a small example of freedom of choice, it is not difficult to relate this type of freedom of awareness and action to greater choices in your life, such as type of work, choice of mate, location of home.

Opening up one's perception of the world can sometimes be a bit frightening. Some of us only know a sick yet comforting level of fear and paranoia. To wake up one morning and *not* feel it might be scary. That is where courage comes in. And that is where the support of others in recovery comes in. There are so many millions beating back this disease from their everyday behavior and consciousness that one never has to be alone. It feels much better to have others along for the ride, to check our behavior and progress with those who are also willing to show courage, commitment, and change.

Let's go back to the subject of willpower. When willing our attitudes to change doesn't work the addictive cycle of low self-esteem, negative thinking, and acting continues. It is important to realize that changing one's attitude and outlook on life comes not as a result of willing ourselves to change, but as a result of doing some hard soul-searching work. That is what the Eighth Step of Alcoholics Anonymous affords us.

Being *willing* to make a list of persons whom we have harmed and consider making amends to them denote the very shift that we desire. The Step of creating the list and being willing to do something about it is the action portion, or the work necessary, to attain the attitude shift.

Overcoming Shame and Guilt

Thinking about those we have harmed takes us out of the victim role and places us in the perpetrator role. It is important to work the Eighth Step with a seasoned sponsor because here is where many people stumble into the guilt and shame caused by this disease. Professionals hear of how so many well-intentioned people in recovery get to Step Five and simply stop doing the work! The fear of the rest of the journey due to shame and guilt is just that huge. But true perpetrators are not puppets, as we are to this disease. Under the influence of chemicals and the lifestyle surrounding them, we have indeed harmed others. The way out of the resulting shame and guilt is presented clearly in these Steps. And the end result is detailed in the Eighth Promise, especially as it relates to how we view ourselves.

The attitude change that begins to happen at about this point in our recovery journey can also be attributed to the action we have taken so far; if we have worked through or avoided shame and guilt, if we have taken responsibility for our actions and have shown care and concern for ourselves by readiness to take action, then our perception of ourselves has already changed. It has changed from a standpoint of having low or no self-esteem, being unworthy of living a life clean of guilt, shame, and ghosts of the past due to harm caused others, to one of being worth living a life that is guilt- and shame-free.

We deserve to live guilt- and shame-free. We did not choose the genes and social circumstances that manifested this disease in us. We did not cause ourselves to become sick. If there were a cure, we would have been the first in line to try it out. Like all people, we have a birthright to be whole, self-actualized people.

At some point in our lives, the disease did arise. Biological, social, genetic, and psychological circumstances all came together to feed the propensity for this disease to manifest itself in our actions. And we became its puppet. It is ridiculous, when we are clearheaded, to think that because of this we need to continually punish ourselves with a polluted, twisted belief system that was based and perfected by a disease that we are the unwitting hosts of.

Alcoholics and addicts are the beautiful people. We are born sensitive by nature. We have the ability to contribute incredible gifts to the world that we live in. Although the act of feeding our addiction harmed the world around us, it isn't too late to make change. Those of us who have been able to enjoy the

Eighth Promise of Sobriety can attest that it is never too late to begin doing the work of changing one's attitude. We know that our new way of seeing the world supports our sobriety and helps us develop the greatest parts of who we really are. It also helps us make easy those things which used to seem so chaotic, so difficult.

Turning Around the Craziness

The disease would have us live in chaos, making simple tasks difficult, catching people in a vortex of craziness around our lives. Recovery from this disease is a process of turning around the craziness. This turnaround can be seen in the following story:

Once upon a time, there was a fellow named Jack, who lived with his wife, Jill, of many years in a town far away. Jack and Jill ran a ranch that barely supported itself, except for the few products that Jack got from his farm animals and the magnificent pasta noodles that Jill made in their kitchen. Things would have been just fine, except that the two argued constantly to the point of wanting to give up their marriage, because Jill's pasta had to be stretched from one end of the kitchen in the small house to the other, taking up space that Jack needed. There wasn't money enough to make the house bigger so that both could have their way. Jill seemed a bit more content than Jack to live with things as they were. But day after day, Jack steamed inside. He was convinced that he lived in hell and it was his own home, the home that was too small.

Jack got to talking with a neighbor over at the next ranch and began for the hundredth time to relate his troubles about having a home that was too small and all the problems it was causing his relationship. The neighbor said, "Hey, why don't you go see the wise woman in the next town. She might be able to help you." Jack had never heard of such a thing as asking for help for personal, private problems, but the suggestion registered in his memory and came up many times during the next few weeks, as he and Jill fought relentlessly over the space problem.

One day, after a particularly bad argument, Jack recalled his neighbor's suggestion. He reluctantly and skeptically made his way into the next town to see about what this wise woman had to say. He expected her to take his money and dole out some kind of ridiculous spell or pronouncement and then he would get back to his life of living in the too small house, miserable as usual. On his way over, he had already decided that nothing would help, but still he found his feet headed in her direction. He knew that he and Jill had already tried just about everything they knew to make the house feel bigger, to stop the fighting between them over space. He did feel a bit desperate for some relief from the old way of doing things.

Jack found the wise woman's house and knocked on her door, still thinking skeptical, cynical thoughts. The woman greeted him, invited him inside, and listened carefully to his problem. She said, "I think I can help you with this problem, Jack. But you have to do exactly as I say, step by step, for this problem of your small house to be resolved." He agreed, but inside he held on to his doubts.

"Well then, the first step that I want you to take is to go back to your ranch and get the rooster. Put the rooster in your house, live with him for a whole week, and come back to see me the following Monday."

Jack saw absolutely no sanity in this woman's advice and he wasted no time in telling her so.

"You already know how to deal with this problem your way. I'm merely suggesting that you try something different," she said.

Jack went back to the ranch and put his rooster in the house. He lived with the rooster for an entire week. It crowed in the morning and woke him up. It startled and jumped about and clucked; it sat on his footrest and distracted him. Its dander and feathers seemed to be everywhere, annoying him. Jill's noodles still stretched from the kitchen to the opposite end of the house, entrapping and aggravating Jack even more than the rooster's presence did.

The following Monday, Jack rushed to the wise woman's home in the next town. He did not expect to hear the next round of her advice.

"Put your goat in your house along with your rooster, Jack."

"This is insane, I won't do it," he protested.

"What is insane is that you have tried many things over and over and you are still living in such a small house. But if you don't want my help . . ." The wise woman began to close her door.

"No, wait. I'll do it," said Jack, trying not to recall how much smaller the house was with the rooster in it, and now with the goat too . . . well, something had to happen. He went to the ranch, pulled the goat into the house, and lived with Jill and her noodles, the rooster, and the goat for an entire week. At the end of the week, just before he went off to see the wise woman, he took stock of his situation.

The goat was noisy and very destructive, eating everything in sight. Drapes, noodles, upholstery, and anything else he could find. It didn't smell so good to be in the house with ranch animals, either. Jill and he fought terribly, even more than before, because there was absolutely no room in the small place to move about. The rooster was generally annoying and messy, aggravating the problems created by the goat. This was not working. Jack was more frustrated than ever. He had even less faith in the wise woman's advice than ever and he ran to the next town to tell her just what he thought about her help.

He knocked on her door, angrily. He shouted at her that his problem had seemed to get worse and that he was going back to the ranch and pulling out the animals. She was a quack, he yelled. She said, "Okay, Jack, have it your way. Good-bye." Then she began to close the door. As she did, a feeling of dread came over him. He remembered that for many years he had tried everything he knew to resolve his problem with the size of the house. He didn't know what else to do but what he had been told to do by the wise woman, and now even this didn't seem to work! He asked her to give him a minute to think, and she did. He couldn't go back, and it seemed nearly impossible to go forward. He felt very stuck, very helpless.

"I give up," he said to her as she stood in the doorway. "I can't fix this problem by myself," he added.

"So, Jack, I see we are making progress. Let's take another step." And then she directed him to go back to his ranch and put his cow into the small house, together with the rooster and the goat and his wife and her long noodles.

Jack and Jill squeezed by the cow, the goat, and the rooster single file to get from the living room to the bedroom and back to the kitchen. There was positively, absolutely no room whatsoever remaining in the house to do anything. The air was thick with animal scent, the sound of animals who were just as uncomfortable as their human hosts, and the entire situation could not get any worse.

Slowly over the week, Jill and Jack found ways to talk to one another when they had to, sometimes by shouting over the animals, sometimes with hand signals. They clung to one another at night because otherwise they would awaken to find their arms around a furry or feathered animal. The scent of Jill was far more preferable than that of Bessie, the cow, after all. Crowding into a corner of the kitchen with her was far more preferable than squeezing into his easy chair with the paper when the chair had been occupied by a rooster and tattered and torn up by the goat.

The following Monday came more quickly than Jack had thought it would. He was eager to see what the wise woman next wanted him to do. He knocked on the door and eagerly asked for his next assignment with all the excitement of a schoolboy.

"Jack, I can see that there has been a change in you during this past week. For your next step, I want you to go back and pull the rooster, the goat, and the cow out of your home. If you feel the need to come back and see me, of course, I'd love to hear what happens."

And that is exactly what Jack did.

The next day, Jack knocked on the wise woman's door. She opened it to see him looking very relaxed and happy, and noted that he held a large bowl of fragrant, long noodles out to her.

"What is this? A gift?"

"Yes, wise woman. It is from Jill and me, to thank you from the bottom of our hearts for all that you have done for us."

"Why I'm not aware that I've done anything at all. I think you have done all the work," she smiled.

"Oh you've done something all right. You've gotten me to see that we live in a house that is big enough for everything we need it for. And for that, we wish you just as much happiness."

"And you were able to see this the moment you pulled out the cow, the goat, and the rooster, right?" asked the wise woman.

"No, come to think of it, I was able to first see how large my house was the moment that I thought I had a problem and admitted that I had been defeated by it."

"Good work, Jack," said the wise woman. She enjoyed the extra-long noodles later that afternoon when Jack had returned to enjoy the spaciousness of his own home.

A Change in Perception

Our journey into recovery works similarly to the tale of Jack and his house, especially as this story relates to the Eighth Promise of Sobriety. Although this story is very rich in a variety of recovery-related elements, let's review just a few for now.

First, Jack's conviction that the problem he and Jill were having was due to the size of the house prevented him from seeing the solution: He was stuck in his way of thinking.

Second, the problem had to persist for a long time and get so bad that it nearly ruined everything the two people had worked so hard for. Addiction is exactly like that.

Then, in a moment of desperation, Jack was forced to act uncharacteristically by actually talking with someone about his problem. In this case, a local rancher. Normally, he would keep his problem a secret. Millions of recovering people can relate to keeping their problem a secret at any cost, only speaking to someone when it seemed that the worst was at hand.

Another thing tying this story to the Eighth Promise is that Jack became willing to seek help and, although skeptical and reluctant, put one foot in front of the other, took each step as it was suggested, even though it made no logical sense to him. Jack had developed a sense of *faith*.

Next, Jack surrendered to the magnitude of the situation before him, admitting that he was powerless over the problem and the solution. That is when his whole attitude began to change.

Finally, with great willingness (unlike the attitude he brought to the wise woman's door at first), he is not given but actually eagerly seeks out the wise woman's final direction. As a result, his outlook on life changes. Suddenly that which used to be too small is quite the right size. And the very skills that he had used to negotiate his problems while taking the steps were the skills that made peace between he and his wife. Jack completes the story with an act of gratitude and acknowledgment of the transition that he has made.

Note that in this story, the house itself never changes. We can hypothesize that this might mean that Jack and Jill's needs and personalities don't change, the size of the house doesn't change, the natures of the barnyard animals don't change, and so on. *The only thing that changes is Jack's perception due to a change he was able to make in himself.* And this is precisely the way that the Eighth Promise of Sobriety works. It doesn't say, "Our world changes"; it says, "Our whole attitude and outlook upon life will change." And for millions, it has.

To review the Eighth Promise of Sobriety:

⁓We can make a tremendous transition by working the Eighth Step in order to achieve the gift described in the Eighth Promise.

⁓It is important to realize that old belief systems that no longer serve us well need to be reevaluated in order to realize the Eighth Promise.

⁓We need help from others to avoid losing ground due to shame and guilt. Alcoholics and addicts are the beautiful people, just as entitled to live guilt- and shame-free as others are.

⁓Our whole attitude and outlook upon life changes when we stop believing that willpower is the answer to our problems. Instead, we surrender to the magnitude of the problem and utilize courage and commitment to cause change.

CHAPTER NINE
Fear of People and of Economic Insecurity Will Leave Us

Today I vow to live cleanly—in the sense that I will enjoy the feeling of lightness that comes from having made things right between me and others who have been in my life. I will enjoy this day because I know that I am safely held by the strong, yet invisible hands of a network of interconnected people, all who have respect for me because I have taken care of the wreckage of my past. I will use today to continue to live without fear of being caught or found out, for there is nothing to discover as I live openly and honestly. I will enjoy the sense of security that I feel knowing that as a part of humanity, not special or separate from it, all of my needs will be taken care of in their right time.

The Ninth Step of Alcoholics Anonymous says, "Made direct amends to such people wherever possible, except when to do so would injure them or others." The Ninth Promise says, "Fear of people and of economic insecurity will leave us." To connect Step Nine with Promise Nine, we need to revisit the idea that the Steps of AA can be viewed as trail markers along a path, and the Promises can be seen as the destination of that path.

With this knowledge, we can see that Step Nine asks us to do some work based on the previous Step, where we are asked to make a list of those we have harmed and check into our level of willingness to make amends to them. Make no mistake, this is no small task. Facing the reality of what the disease has wrought in our lives through recognizing the pain we have caused others is very frightening. No small coincidence, then, that Promise Nine addresses one of the most universal fears of us all: economic insecurity.

Economic insecurity touches upon all of our most basic and primordial fears. Fear of not having enough money affects nearly every area of our lives. As far as the disease of addiction goes, guaranteeing a steady stream of money is just as important as guaranteeing a steady supply of alcohol or drugs. Therefore, we will go to any lengths to get our drink or drug, and unfortunately these lengths usually involve manipulating, using, taking advantage of, and harming other people.

The Power of Making Amends

Here is how one man, a physician, handled making his amends. He had been brought up to the medical board and told that if he went to treatment, he would be able to keep his license to practice medicine. A family program was part of the treatment program, and his entire family participated fully. Here is what happened after treatment, as the man worked his way through the Steps to the Ninth Step of AA:

"From a personal standpoint, I think that a lot of the gifts of sobriety have to do with making amends, especially as regards lessening the fear of economic insecurity. My family is very accepting of what was going on. That didn't happen very often. It was accepted that this was a disease, but still none of us understood It very well. I felt like I needed to sit down and make amends to them fairly soon after. Within the next six to eight months I sat down with my wife and then with my kids separately and made amends. I thought that this was a fairly formal process. I don't know if they had that same perception or not.

"I made amends to my children one by one. One was in college, one was out working, and one was in another college, so it was sort of separate. When I made amends, I was hopeful but I didn't have expectations that it was going to turn out well. But it did. I made amends to my old business manager. She didn't work for us anymore, but back then I had fired her one day and then called her up the next day and rehired her. But I asked her to come to the office and sat down and told her that I was in recovery. I told her first of all that she was a good business manager. I just apologized for the things that I had done. She blew it all off. She said, 'That's life.' I never understood her reaction to it. But I felt like I needed to do that. It was good for me.

"The feelings that I had after I made amends were relief that I was through with that loop so to speak. In a way it was putting an end to that chapter of my life. I didn't need to explain so much as close the books and leave that part behind me. They were very forgiving and glad that this part was over in their minds. Best of all, I was able to maintain my ability to practice medicine and I have not been at all insecure about money. The amends helped me to focus on what is important in life, not on earning a living. With the support of my family and friends, I could remain sober and retain my medical practice, thus maintaining a sense of security. Sobriety helps me focus on the right goal. The right goal was my support network, not struggling with the board to maintain my income."

The Clutch of Guilt and Shame

When we are under the influence of mood-altering chemicals, we are literally out of our minds. Actions that would be abhorrent to us while sober are of little or no significance when we are not sober. It is difficult to follow a code of ethics when we have no way of making a healthy connection with others, and we have lost connection with a power greater than ourselves. Worse, the people most harmed are often those to whom we are closest.

Step Nine and Promise Nine are designed to intervene on the process of harming others in the service of gaining a steady stream of support for the disease. Step Nine and Promise Nine also address not only the need to stop harming others, but also our willingness to stop harming ourselves through bearing feelings of embarrassment, guilt, and shame due to harm we have caused, in the past, via the disease.

The Step and the Promise are perfectly matched so that we might soon know the gift of our birthright as human beings: to live with love and happiness, to live without fear, to feel a part of all things, to feel confident and secure.

Many of us have allowed the cycle of addiction to spin around us and tighten into a choke-hold unchecked because we fear facing the reality of our actions while actively addicted. The longer the cycle is allowed to continue, the more likely the disease is to strengthen Itself using the healthy resources of others. This is such a powerfully destructive force that even if the disease manages to kill Its host, It can persist and grow in those who were connected with the deceased, even if they are not chemically dependent.

To deal with such a powerful force, a powerful intervention is required. With all of the preparation of the Steps behind it, that powerful force comes from our willingness to take deliberate actions to make our present-day experience free from guilt and shame. The Ninth Promise says that we will not have to go through our days worrying about getting our basic needs met. Preparing for and then making amends to those we have harmed allows for these two types of fears to dissipate over time.

This particular Promise is perhaps the most lauded, the most talked about, the one that seems so magical to those who begin to feel relief from their fears about people and money. These fears are primary and are based on basic human needs. Most of us are entirely driven to take care of the need for belonging socially, as well as for obtaining food, shelter, water, and so on. Ironically, the very thing that we grow to fear—people—is also the key to growing and staying out of fear. This is a very clear example of how the disease turns everything inside out in an Alice in Wonderland sort of way.

The disease is so effective in supporting Itself because It latches on to our most primal and primary needs and makes Itself appear to be a necessary part of obtaining these needs. That is why we can observe others who are caught up in the addiction cycle changing their ethics and morals so readily. Their vision of how to get one's needs met becomes skewed, and, sadly, the other part of the disease is that It covers up their own knowledge of the negative transformation.

But the Ninth Promise tells us that at some point, we will not have a fear about economics. We will feel secure. How can this be? It happens because, with sobriety, we are able to truly connect with ourselves, with others, and with a power greater than ourselves. When we reconnect with ourselves and our feelings, we feel our own power. When we reconnect with others, we feel secure. When we are able to admit our place in the universe, however small or large, by identifying a Higher Power, we can maintain a sense of wholeness inside since we have now become a part of a wholeness outside and all around us.

Blessings in Unlikely Circumstances

Here is a story to illustrate what happens when the Ninth Step has been worked and the Ninth Promise has come true. As you read this story, ask yourself what you might do under these circumstances. What might your family and friends have advised you? Would you have taken that advice?

"Now I have been sober many years, and have worked the Steps over and over again, never seeing anything that looked like as much evidence of my spiritual progress as what happened to me on this one particular day. I was able to behave entirely differently than I had ever behaved before, and I owe it to my years of sobriety. Here is what happened: I was on my way to work one day when something interesting happened to me. I had just started a new job and was making my way down the highway when I was broadsided on the right by an old car that seemed to be entirely out of control. My car veered at top speed into the opposite lane of traffic. I couldn't brake and the steering didn't seem to work. I was screaming at the top of my lungs because I was sure I was about to die.

"In fact, I saw the oncoming traffic headed straight for me, and one man threw his hands over his face just before we were supposed to hit, head-on. But somehow, we didn't hit. My car swerved to the left, hit the opposite side of the street's curb, and ran its wheels along the curb around the corner. Then suddenly, my car stopped neatly and parked itself. I looked down at my legs. There was only upholstery. I panicked and put my hands on my thighs. My legs slowly materialized in what seemed like granules. My body felt fine, although I was shaken up and my heart was pounding out of extreme fright.

"The car that had hit me had kept on going down the highway, but many people ran over to help me. I got out of the car, noting that I felt just fine. I wondered if I was in shock. Earlier that morning, I had gone for a two-mile run in some old sneakers that made my right lower back hurt. On my way home from work, I was going to buy some new sneakers to solve the problem. I noticed that my lower back wasn't hurting any longer. In fact, I felt rather energized and somehow more than fine. Certainly it was because of the adrenaline, I thought.

"A police officer arrived on the scene immediately. He called the paramedics to make sure I was okay, but there was nothing for them to do since I felt great. I was so happy to be alive. Many people had seen the accident and were talking all at once to the officer taking the report. They told him that they saw two cars headed straight for one another but nothing happened. In fact, there were no skid marks where they obviously were going to collide. The only proof that the incident happened at all was a long tire mark on the side of the curb on the opposite side of the highway. The officer called my boss to tell him that I would be in shortly.

"The man who had hit me was caught about a mile up the road by two other officers who chased him. The man had been in a state of diabetic shock. They had to pry his fingers from the steering wheel and feed him something before he came out of his catatonic state. When they told him what he had done, he was horrified and asked them to take him back to where I was. The man begged forgiveness. He said he should not have been driving with his condition, but he had no other way to get around. He said not to worry about anything, that he would take care of everything. He said he had plenty of money even though he had no car insurance. I looked at the police officer who said, 'I think he's on the level, which is good because your car is a mess.' Actually, my car was totaled.

"The next few days passed and I felt better and better both inside and outside. I had no whiplash, no headaches, no body aches, nothing. Instead, I felt energized, uplifted, and grateful. I called the man who hit me and told him that if he could write me a check for the value of my car plus enough to help me get into another car, I'd consider the entire issue closed. He was amazed, and we made plans to meet the next day.

"Meanwhile, my friends told me that I should sue this man for every dollar he had and then some. They told me that he could have killed me or someone else, that he had no business being on the road, and that I could be a very rich woman if I'd only take care of myself. But I couldn't do it. I couldn't even think of it. I decided not to listen to them.

"I met this man at his home. He wrote me a check for more than my car was worth plus a few thousand extra to take care of having to get another car. The man tore up his driver's license in front of me and told me he had sold his car for one dollar to a needy family. He bought a senior citizen bus pass and would not be driving ever again. I offered to take him to the store or, if he was in a pinch, he could call me for a ride now and then, as I worked not far from his home. We wished each other well and said good-bye. Only two pieces of paper exchanged hands: a check from him to me and a paper from me to him stating I would not sue him for the accident. We hugged one another. He said he was so grateful that I was not harmed.

"At first I looked at gigantic trucks to buy, thinking that after an accident like the one I had been through, one couldn't be too careful. But then I recalled how I was headed straight for that man who had raised his hands in horror over his face. I recalled how my car seemed to park itself safely in a parallel parking spot. I remembered how my legs appeared under my hands when at first there was nothing to see but the seat. And I also thought about how good my back felt, how it had been adjusted properly by the kinetic force of being hit on the right side by a big old car. I knew that God had everything to do with this incident and that the type of car or metal that I had been in had nothing to do with my state of being.

"I went around the corner from the truck dealer and bought the tiniest sports car I could find. That accident was a blessing to me. I am grateful that it happened. It obviously needed to happen.

"There was a time, before I understood what a spiritual program was, that I would have refused to speak to the man who hit me. I would have demanded a copy of the police report and called my insurance company on the spot. I would have tried to sue that man for every penny that could be gotten without regard for his well-being or his family.

"I am grateful for being in recovery. My gift of sobriety is that without a fear of poverty, I am free to see the blessings in even the most traumatic events. My sobriety has changed the way that I look at everything I do and reaffirmed my sense of connection with other people. I no longer feel that people are out to get me and I, in return, am no longer out to get anybody, either. I was able to trust my intuition, to trust my own sense of right and wrong, which is a real big deal after screwing up for so many years on that subject. Even though my friends advised me to hire lawyers and go after the assets of the man who ran his car into mine, I was free to make the right decision, and the result to the both of us, as well as others that might be affected by this man's health problems in the future, is positive."

The gift of sobriety here is not simply the unusual outcome of the physical aspects of the accident, but the interpersonal dealings between the fellow who ran into this woman's car, and the woman's conduct herself after the accident. With complete faith that she would be taken care of, not only by the man who ran his car into hers but by the world as a whole, the woman was able to see where humanity, true justice, and responsibility should be.

To wake up in the morning with gratitude for being given just one more sober day is often all it takes to put a smile and a sense of accomplishment in a recovering person's heart. Since early on, this is accomplished through prayer and meditation and meetings, the remainder of the day is to marvel in what occurs when this bountiful feeling is shared with others. Through giving to others in some way, one realizes just how fortunate one truly is. This is why fear of economic insecurity leaves us. We are not focused on economic security any longer! Our security does not come from taking from others but from giving. With sobriety the energy is reversed, the looking glass effect is corrected, right thinking is established or re-established. We are focused on staying clean and sober, working a good program, living in the moment, taking care of our business, and providing the world with service. The cycle increases and our newly defined wealth increases as well.

When Less Is More

Here, another recovering person shares how he enjoys the Ninth Promise of Sobriety:

"I used to dream, day in and day out, of making a lot of money and of living free of problems because someday, in the distant future, I would have so much money that I could buy my way out of anything. I could buy freedom; I would be the most attractive partner to someone else; I could live in luxury and have all of my many needs met. I worked hard toward this dream. Using drugs supported working harder and harder, and soon I was working harder to earn more money to support my addiction. There is an old saying that goes, 'The man takes a drink, the drink takes a drink, the drink takes the man.' This is so true! I was living in the future and my future robbed my ability to enjoy the minute-by-minute present.

"After many tries and failures, I managed to establish some years of sobriety and, with it, a good spiritual program. I decided that, as wacky as it seemed, I would never charge for my services when I counseled, but I would only ask for donations. I never knew from one day to the next how much money my labors would bring me, and I gave up thinking about it. I used an old coffee can with a hole in the plastic lid. I opened it up after each individual session or each group and found that, more often than not, it contained just what I needed when all was said and done. I had learned complete surrender, humility, had contained my great desires to accumulate more and more and more things, and instead recalibrated my definitions of happiness and purpose and meaning to be in direct proportion to the depth of strong, honest interpersonal connections. I gave of myself freely, and I was given to freely in return, without expectation. In other words, I gave up trying to control things so that I could most certainly make enough money each month and year. I realized that when I controlled this, I was always left wanting, never satisfied.

"Often, I was more and more behind than ahead just because of the thought process that goes with trying for this fallacy called security! I simply decided to give that definition up entirely. That is when I really began to prosper. Because, you see, prospering has very little to do with earning a lot of money. Prospering to me means thriving energetically on moment-to-moment life as it is given, in the best of health and relationships with others. Paradoxically, I now make more money than I ever have in my entire life because I do what I love to do without any regard for what monetary gains I get or lose. Money is no longer a motivation. I am glad to have discovered this when I did. Had I been active in my addiction, I would never have had the presence of mind to be able to learn this neat little trick that has been one of the very best gifts of my entire sobriety!"

To review the Ninth Promise of Sobriety:
~The Ninth Step and the Ninth Promise are paired to suggest the direction we should take in order to enjoy the gifts of the Promise.
~The Promise of losing our fear of people and economic insecurity is an important one, as we were not meant to live a life full of guilt, shame, and embarrassment.
~This Promise celebrates the turning around from insecurity to security—a straightening of one's perception of economics from greed to gratitude.
~The concept of a power greater than ourselves is important in terms of realizing the gifts of security.
~Changing perception thanks to sobriety has a great humanizing and loving effect on our world—family, community, friends, and significant others.
~Chasing after economic security, paradoxically, has an opposite effect. Serving others brings economic security with surety.

CHAPTER TEN
We Will Intuitively Know How to Handle Situations Which Used to Baffle Us

Today I am grateful for the gifts of my sobriety that have increasingly come to me over time: the return of my own wisdom and clear intuition.

At first it is difficult to believe that anything will lift the misery that comes from being addicted. But once you've received even a hint of the first of the gifts that sobriety has to offer, the rest begin to arrive and be realized sooner and faster. We just need practice, with a clean and sober mind available to us, in learning how to see, feel, hear, taste, and otherwise intuit everything all over again. Like learning to ride a bicycle, it doesn't take long before everything recalibrates and experiencing the gifts becomes as normal as moving upright, in a forward direction, on only two skinny little wheels.

At first we may feel baffled. It seems that everybody has an opinion about our sobriety, doesn't it? Our significant other, our doctor, our friends, our spiritual advisors or religious leaders, our children, advertising, commercials—all have The Way pointed out for us.

And then, there is the way that we wish to go, and yet we know that every single time we go our own way, follow our intuition or our best thinking, we wind up either back where we were, or worse. More promises to our loved ones are broken. More shame brought upon ourselves. More illness, less ability to cover up the signs of our drinking and using. Each time we attempt to stop the cycle wrought by the disease by ourselves, using our very best thinking, we somehow fail. We feel embarrassed that something seemingly so simple as not uncorking the wine bottle, not spending all that energy, risk, and money buying or stealing drugs always backfires on us. We blame others, we blame the universe, we blame circumstances, starting sentences out with "If only . . ." or "It wouldn't have happened except for . . ." but inside we know we are helpless over this thing that keeps growing inside of us. The first thing we must do is give up our struggle with this thing that is so great that we continue to lose to it. But giving up, we have been taught, is wrong.

Think about it: A captain goes down with his ship. A good soldier stays with his men even in the face of annihilation. Giving up is for losers. These are things we are taught. And we get these messages in a variety of ways well before we even learn how to speak. They are so much a part of us that it is very difficult to see that we have the right and the ability to discard these ideas if we so choose.

And yet, discarding belief systems such as these is necessary in order to take the first steps toward real sobriety. So many things we believe in need to be turned around, such as the idea that one wins by never giving in. With this disease, paradoxically speaking, one actually has to lose to win. We must give in to give up our drug and alcohol habit. And we need to *quit trying* to give up the struggle in order to actually give it up.

Being Beyond a Ninety-Day Wonder

A recovering man describes how this Promise enhances his life and how he understands it:

"I used to be baffled by the concept of spirituality. And so I went on a kind of spiritual quest. Along the way, I met a guy who would come into and out of AA. We called him a 'ninety-day wonder.' He'd become a spiritual giant about once every ninety days; then he would drop out of the program and drink again. About that time, I happened to read something that said, 'You cannot be spiritual and know it.' Between the 'ninety-day wonder' guy and that single concept about how paradoxical chasing spirituality is, I was no longer baffled by the concept. I now have faith and trust that when it is time for me to understand something, the understanding will come to me in its own sweet time and not because I want it to happen on my own terms.

"Here is something I know how to handle that I did not know how to handle before, thanks to the slow reemergence of more subtle functions that I lost while drinking. My intuition was given back to me, and I was able to solve a puzzle about spirituality that, twenty years ago, would have baffled me. My intuition is a true gift. Life is lived more fully with the addition of it."

Once these concepts have been understood through giving in and giving up and losing over and over and over again, the Tenth Promise begins to emerge in ever greater force. The mystery of why we could never achieve self-esteem, real belief in ourselves, genuine trust of ourselves and others, true economic security, and expertise in any one area begins to unfold. With sobriety, our health begins to return. Our brain begins the healing process. As each cell compensates and generates new balanced communications to the next cell in the process of healing, our thinking clears up. We begin to feel as if we are standing on ever more solid ground. Day after day of sobriety brings increasing clarity and with it the ability to learn.

The Tenth Step of Alcoholics Anonymous says, "Continued to take personal inventory and when we were wrong promptly admitted it." What we learn through the Tenth Step is that as human beings, we are fallible and we have great big egos. Even though we have made amends once, we need to continually take inventory of ourselves and, as stated above, repeatedly lose this egocentricity by admitting our mistakes. In this way, we continually drop off the baggage of embarrassment, guilt, and shame. With no burden to drag into the present and the future, we are free to learn. The more we learn, the more we realize how to handle things that used to baffle us. Relationship problems that occurred and recurred even though we would change people, places, and things begin to resolve themselves. It is because we aren't taking the past into the present. We are using the Tenth Step to create the Tenth Promise.

Here is the story of a man who now has a good handle on his life thanks to following instructions rather than staying in the proverbial driver's seat and trying to manage his own early recovery:

"I went through treatment, a year of continuing care, and all the things that one is asked to do when one enters treatment. I got a bachelor's degree and the opportunity to work on a master's degree. I have three children who I know now that I did not know before, as well as six grandchildren. I got all of that family that I did not have before. I got the opportunity to stop trying to commit suicide, stop doing something called death, and begin to do something called life. The Promises came true for me because my sobriety gave me back choice in my life. I now have choices instead of single items to focus my attention on.

"I was given the opportunity to find the kind of work that I like to do, as opposed to the type of work that I was supposed to do. I got the chance to stop spending all that money on booze. This was more beneficial for me and for my family. Sobriety gave me the ability to reengage in a marriage which at that point was in its twenty-third year. It brought me the gift of being able to know how to talk with my wife, to learn how to listen to one another, and to be together. I've also gotten the opportunity to look at some old wounds, some pain that came at one time, the abandonment issues from having a parent die early, and I've had a chance to look at some of those things as to how they have affected me later on in life. These things are affecting me now, thirteen years into my sobriety. I'm probably dealing better with them now than I did before, but the opportunity to continue to look at these issues is there. So I get to look at these things, make some decisions, make some choices, go through some pain, and do just what I want to do: grow."

Growth and Change

The Tenth Step and the Tenth Promise talk about this very subject. Growth. One of the character defects that many of us find while we are working Steps Four through Seven is a distinct lack of humility. Without humility there can be no growth. The system laid out in the Steps is to introduce a concept, prepare us to work through the concept, and then suggest a way to do this work. In order to enjoy the gift of the Tenth Promise, then, each of the Steps leading up to the Tenth Step must be worked in earnest. There are no shortcuts, no speedy thirty-day Twelve Step process. While each of us makes progress as we can, this progress takes differing amounts of time. It took a long, long time to develop a drug and/or alcohol problem the size of which concerns us or those we love. It will take just as long, if not longer, to work our way back to trust, self-love, and health.

Now what about this thing that we need in order to grow and change so that we are able to send this awful disease into remission? We must have humility in order to respect our enemy properly. If we do not respect the power of our enemy, the disease, It conquers us over and over again. Reaching a state of humility in the face of a powerful enemy allows us to take a step back and look at the disease as It is, not as we wish It might be. This is an adult way to handle a problem. While we are actively drinking or using drugs, we can't be objective. We are actually in part of the problem, and therefore we cannot see the true size of it, much less stand apart from it and see its weaknesses as well as its strengths. While we are actively under the influence of Its power, we are conquered. The process of achieving a solid, trustworthy state of long-term abstinence from drugs and alcohol begins with our initial sobriety.

Reaching a state of humility in the face of this disease means being willing to stop falsely inflating ourselves so that we don't feel small relative to others. It means being willing to say, "I don't know." Most important, it means being willing and ready to admit that we need help. It establishes the fact that we are not able to get well alone.

Once this key fact has been accepted and established, we need to be willing to constantly look at ourselves and our behavior and be responsible for slips that harm others. Old habits die hard, as the saying goes, and just because we aren't drinking or using any longer doesn't mean that we aren't prone to lie, manipulate, or use other behaviors to get our way. Our unwillingness to review and change this behavior leads to relapse in the long term, but in the short term it blocks the development of our much-needed support system.

So the Tenth Step helps us leave behind well-practiced and well-developed behaviors and actions, in addition to helping us constantly mend fences in our support system. The disease, although inactive, still has the power to cause us to self-destruct by disappointing our friends and family with old behaviors. When these old behaviors become magnified enough to wreak obvious havoc on our lives, it can be said that we are experiencing what is called dry drunk behavior. The substance has been removed; however, the behaviors are in full force.

Ego Management

The Tenth Promise, "We will intuitively know how to handle situations that used to baffle us," addresses the effective application of the Tenth Step in that by continuing to take personal inventory and promptly admitting when we were wrong, we are keeping our willingness large and our egos small. We need to be humble enough to make room for new information. Humility will help us experience the pleasure of support from those who are willing to forgive us and drop their resentments toward our difficult, defensive behavior. Humility will help us accept the tools to beat this disease into remission—if only we stop sending our helpers away with overly knowledgeable remarks, slights, insults, one-upmanship, competitiveness, and manipulations.

Best of all, it is never too late to clean up each large and small mess we create as we make mistakes along the way. The Tenth Step allows us our humanity and allows us a way not to suffer or have others suffer very long for our need to learn. Because we are not creating insurmountable mountains of problems before we shrink these into tiny molehills, the healing, learning, growing process is manageable and accessible, even to those of us who nearly kill ourselves or ruin the lives of others because of the disease.

In this way the Tenth Promise can be realized. In a different way and at a different time, each of us sees the signs that we are beginning to receive the gift of the return of our intuition and insight, of our own truth and wisdom. It takes from one to three years for the brain to recover, depending on many factors (length of use, genetics, amount of use, and so on). And it is easy to become discouraged when we see other recovering people progressing while we feel that our own efforts are causing us to backslide. We have to be kind to ourselves as much as we are concerned about being kind to those who are supporting us in spite of what damage the disease may have brought into our life. We have to take our own inventory daily, often hourly, and when we find something awry, fix it as soon as possible with a heartfelt apology, regardless of how others react.

People who do not grow up as addicts or alcoholics go through the various stages of infancy, childhood, adolescence, and early adulthood with a clear mind. As they experiment with certain behaviors, they see which ones work and which ones don't. They fine-tune and recalibrate. They change periodically to maintain connection with others around them. From this process of moving through one stage to the next, gaining information and using this information to change and grow, nonaddicts gain a great deal of wisdom and good judgment. Problems that used to be difficult gradually becomes easy until they are no longer problems at all.

But adults who have the disease of addiction often have a different growth cycle through these same stages that lead to adulthood. Without a clear mind, the brain is preoccupied with maintaining its supply of chemicals. Turned inward upon its own needs, it allows only that growth which hones and refines its singular goal. Situations that baffled us then tended to baffle us over and over through adolescence into early and full adulthood. Until we have that moment of clarity (maybe it has happened while you have been reading this book) that it is the disease Itself, and not us that is sick, until there is a moment of separation, often brought by many moments of desperation, we repeat the same things over and over again.

Recall the definition of insanity: Insanity is doing the same thing again and again while expecting different results. We could say that this is the definition of the entire disease of addiction. This insanity is eclipsed by the Tenth Promise. With growth and change, with a willingness to look repeatedly at ourselves and our actions without dragging guilt and shame along, we, too, can begin to master situations that before were plaguing us as problems over and over again.

To review the Tenth Promise of Sobriety:
～We need to be willing to give up our struggle with the disease in order to see It for what It really is.
～Reevaluating belief systems that keep us from finding new ways to grow and change is necessary to realize the gifts that come with the Tenth Promise.
～We need to lose in order to win.

⁓We need to continually take inventory to stay clear of the baggage of embarrassment, guilt, and shame.

⁓When we are free to learn and grow, we can see new ways to do things that we couldn't see before.

⁓When we gain a sense of humility, we are free to grow and change, further sending the disease into remission.

⁓Addicts and alcoholics may often move through developmental stages (infancy, childhood, adolescence, and so on) differently than those who do not have the disease. Knowing how to handle situations that used to baffle us is how we know that we are living in the adult phase of our lives.

CHAPTER ELEVEN

We Will Suddenly Realize That God Is Doing for Us What We Could Not Do for Ourselves

Higher Power, today I am admitting my powerlessness over this disease. I am praying for knowledge of your will and asking for the power to carry it out.

The Eleventh Promise of Sobriety and the Eleventh Step of Alcoholics Anonymous speak directly to one another in that they both address a single key concept: powerlessness.

The last chapter noted that in order to win, we need to learn how to lose. On the subject of powerlessness (not to be confused with helplessness), this concept is an important one to become acquainted with. The Eleventh Promise begins to come true once we understand and practice a daily routine that includes the idea of losing to win. The Eleventh Step, "Sought through prayer and meditation to improve our conscious contact with God *as we understood Him,* praying only for knowledge of His will for us and the power to carry that out," suggests a way to create this understanding and practice.

The Steps themselves can be thought of as a clarifying and cleansing process. Just as our addictive chemicals need to work their way out of our system, all of the attendant behaviors that supported our addiction also need to work their way out of our lives. The system suggested by the Twelve Steps of AA facilitates a brilliant and direct process. It asks us to first consider our willingness and then to take action on several points that involve accepting the fact that we have a disease and that we cannot heal it by ourselves; then it provides us with a method of healing that encompasses each and every need we will have as we journey toward long-term abstinence. It even tells us what we will get if we are able to maintain willingness and take action over and over again.

One of the most magnificent gifts of sobriety is a clear realization that we are supported in ways we had never even dreamed of. As we grow evermore into our recovery, we are surrounded with like-minded people who help us and whom we gain the pleasure of helping. But we also learn that we have support from a power greater than ourselves, and the full realization of this support is, in and of itself, a very great gift. For many, it is the greatest. For once we realize that this Higher Power is a constant and not a periodic grace in our lives, we can begin to relax and allow things to be as they are. Even the most tense and anxious people make profound change once this Eleventh Promise begins to come true.

A woman who was having some difficulty with anxiety once received a helpful gift from her therapist in the form of a sign that she placed on her refrigerator:

"Good morning. This is God. I will be handling all your problems today. I will not need your help. So have a good day."

Spiritual Baby Steps

While we are actively drinking and using drugs, we may be able to go through the motions of spirituality. We may manage to get to church or temple and avoid scrutiny and social pressure for not doing so. But once there, the actual purpose of and connection between others of our faith or practice can never exist. Spiritual connection with others is impossible while the brain is turned inward, seeking its chemical feeding.

Another relationship that is impossible while we are actively drinking or using drugs is a truthful relationship with God or any semblance of a power greater than ourselves. We cannot hear the voice of our Higher Power in nature, in the signs laid out before us, in the miracles that others are experiencing. We have no ability to deeply care and integrate this into our daily world because, even on the most mechanical, biological level, we are unavailable for such connection.

We are also unavailable for a connection with ourselves when we are actively addicted. We don't need to care, says our brain, since an automatic destruction system is now in charge, and a life full of love, acceptance, peace, serenity, and security is not necessary. Not only is it not necessary, but it is also antithetical to the destructive system that is currently in charge. Any of these gifts, should they suddenly appear, must be destroyed or made to be such a low priority that the destructive system can continue to be primary.

Prayer and meditation are conversations with our Higher Power. Many people, having used or drank for so long, have no relationship with or concept of a Higher Power. Many come from families where the legacy of drinking and chemical use has prevented a concept from forming within the family belief system. Some of us have to actually begin to do the action of praying and meditating long before we even know what it is we want to pray about, or even how to pray.

Sitting quietly for any length of time is a definite challenge for the newly recovering alcoholic/addict. The disease has tinkered with our brains just enough to make the idea of sitting still so threatening as to be anxiety provoking and nearly intolerable. While detoxing, it may be next to impossible to sit still or to tolerate the depression or racing thoughts that occur. It may be ridiculous even to try to do anything but hold on to what small shred of sanity one might have while the chemicals leave our bodies and the disease temporarily wreaks havoc on our mental health.

However, once this period has passed, and it does (but never fast enough for any of us), then there is a period that feels rather unsteady. It is an empty space that is left behind by the insanity and behaviors of active addiction, and an empty space not yet filled up with new knowledge and healthy actions. This is a time when many who are new at sobriety bolt right out the clean and sober door. At least the old way is the known way, they think. The unknown is impossible to deal with, right? Wrong.

Tolerating the unknown is part of recovering from drug and alcohol addiction and involves understanding and negotiating a new state of being that is probably very unlike what we learned growing up. This state is called powerlessness. In other belief systems this powerlessness is sometimes referred to as selflessness. And this is where the concept of "losing" to win comes in. Before we learn how to look forward to or even embrace the unknown, we take baby steps toward accepting the unknown by practicing tolerance of the unpleasant feelings that accompany experiencing something that does not feel "quite right" yet. At first, sobriety feels very strange. We enter it with tolerance and grow this tolerance into joy. But, as is said quite often, "First things first."

When Losing Is the Perfect Strategy

Here is how the concept of powerlessness works: If we are willing to throw in the towel during a fight, then there can be no more fight. If we are willing to let go of our attachment to something, then that thing ceases to have power over us. It really does take "two to tango" when it comes to this addiction. First, a mood-altering chemical, and second, you or me. There must be a willingness to hold on to the world created by chemicals. That world feels as if it is made of control but it is not.

The mirage of an ordered world that addiction throws up on our dream screen is all too much like the gigantic image of Oz before Toto reveals the true nature of the great wizard to be a rather inconsequential, fallible human being. If we are hell-bent on winning the fight against our addiction, we have already lost. The disease wins 100 percent of the time with this method. That is a fact. The uncanny reason why we lose each and every time is that *the disease uses our own strengths to conquer us*. We are fighting ourselves with the best part of ourselves. When it is said that this disease is cunning, baffling, and powerful, it should be noted that It gets Its power to be perfect in Its treachery with our bodies and lives directly from us.

So how do you beat such a perfectly designed enemy? If It thinks like us minus the flaws, if It learns how to perfect and grow in Its abilities like us minus the need for a classroom, books, or a limitation of hours with which to do homework, how is this war "winnable"? The answer is, it is not winnable. And that is why we must "lose" to win. Losing is the perfect strategy in this particular war. If I lose, the spoils of this war are that I get to live. I might even get to have quality in my life if I lose enough and frequently at that. Every time I let my ego get in the way or forget this valuable strategy, I try to win. When I try to win, I am conquered. My quality of life disappears and then my health. Then I disappear permanently.

In Step One, recall that it states, "We admitted we were powerless over alcohol—that our lives had become unmanageable." This is fundamental to the concept of losing to win. We must admit that we have no power over this disease (whether it be via drugs or alcohol or both) and literally give up or lose the battle in order to begin the process of winning it.

When we give in, or lose, we are afforded moments of objectivity that we would not otherwise have. Who we are without the disease and who we are with the disease separates in our view and while it frightens us, it also can liberate us if we will take action. As long as we are battling the disease, trying to overcome It with our willpower, It is in us, using our willpower to conquer us in baffling ways. There are too many times when a friend or family member has seemingly won the battle with alcohol or drugs only to have a violent revisiting of the struggle years later, either for a good reason or no good reason at all. It always begins with "just one." Just one sip, joint, smoke, pop, snort . . . just one innocent, "this one doesn't even barely count" hit, rock, tab, whatever. Maybe not this very day, or next month, but *the end result, if left untreated, is always death.* That is why the American Medical Association termed alcoholism a disease. It fits all of the same criteria that other diseases must meet.

That is why the Eleventh Promise is so important. By the time we can actually "see that God is doing for us what we could not do for ourselves," we are well on our way to restoring our lives in ways that often make many of us grateful that we have this hideous disease in the first place! Many of us say that there would not have been the growth and change, nor the precious transformation from rote living to meaningful, purposeful living had we not been afflicted. For the newly sober, just breathing, standing on our own two feet in an upright position, and not wishing to die is quite enough. And, as the Eleventh Promise points out, as time goes on, the gifts deepen and become ever richer.

Couldn't Live Well, Couldn't Die Well

The woman who tells her story here experienced great pain on her journey toward recovery:

"My story, when I look back at it, is as incredible to me as it may sound to you, and shocking and sad for me to tell to others, still, but in the telling of it I know I'm healing myself, slowly but surely, over the years. I almost want to apologize in advance for telling you about what happened when two of the Promises kicked in for me, but I know that a part of that healing is accepting myself and what happened to me through my drinking and using as something that had to happen, needed to happen, and that I had no control over the events. I have a disease that is cunning, baffling, and powerful, and there is no way that I was then or am now or will ever be big enough or strong enough to take It on.

"Many years ago, when I was still drinking, smoking dope,

and taking any kind of pill that seemed to offer some kind of relief, something happened to me that I will never forget. My mother had had heart problems for some time and a whole host of other health problems, and suddenly she took a turn for the worse and became totally bedridden. It was so hard to see her helpless and in pain. She had really been a rock in our family. My sister and her husband did most of the caretaking and eventually had my mother move in with them when she was too ill to stay in her own home with assistance.

"My mother and I were the best of friends my entire life, and, in fact, we had been drinking buddies of sorts. Sometimes through our drinking, we bonded together so that the others in the family were rendered helpless in terms of interfering with our drinking. We'd just stay up late getting smashed and laugh them off. And if my mother could do that, then so could I. I felt invincible when I was with her. We were so close that she made me promise that when it was time for her to go, she wouldn't die alone. I told her that of course she wouldn't die alone, that I'd be right there with her, and at the time, I meant every word that I said. She did not ask this of anybody but me, and I felt so honored to be that special to her. I didn't want her to die, wasn't looking anywhere near forward to her leaving me, but the reality of it didn't really hit because I was drinking. Even through the worst of her pain, we drank, shared her prescription medications, and laughed things off in a stupor that would have made most other people terribly distraught with grief.

"My sister and her husband left me in charge of my mother when they went away for the evening one night. Mom's health had declined so much by then that it was nonstop discomfort and pain. Her breathing was labored that night, and while I sat next to her on her bed, she whispered to me, 'Remember, you promised not to let me die alone.'

"I sat up and drank and watched TV for a while, and then took one of her valiums and slipped off into a dopey sleep. Next thing I know, my mother was coughing up blood and not a little. She was choking and panicking, looking at me to help her. But I was so drunk and stoned that I just wasn't there. I held her in my arms, thinking that she'd get better any minute, but she didn't. I remember dialing 911 when she began vomiting blood, and I remember holding her in my arms, rocking her. She died in my arms right then and there. And then I blacked out.

"I woke up the next day and everything had been cleaned up. My sister and brother-in-law explained to me every detail of what happened when they came home. I was overcome with grief and sickness and more humiliation and embarrassment all at once than I had ever felt before. I drank some more to get myself under control. How could I have slept through my mother's death? How could I not have known what happened? The way they found us, covered in blood and wrapped up together, with me fallen to the side on the bed with her dead in my arms must have been terrible and shocking. And there I was, sick and unaware of the whole thing when I woke up.

"I was selfish and self-centered as a drunk and a pill-head, but I had dismissed this behavior until my mother's death. Not being able to fully keep my promise, not being able to be responsible in an emergency, and especially for the one most important person in my entire life was like a much-needed slap in the face. That was my bottom. I was so ashamed of myself, felt so hopeless and useless that it only seemed logical to follow my mother. I imagined she was at peace, and I was so tormented by my own self and my actions that I wanted that same kind of peace too.

"I tried to drink and dope myself to death several times, but each time I woke up, sicker than a dog, and very much alive. About the fourth time I tried to put myself to sleep and failed, I woke up sick, but I woke up knowing that death wasn't going to happen at my convenience. That forced me to acknowledge that a power greater than myself was at work in my life. It just wasn't my time to go, no matter how hard I tried to kill myself. Yet I did not know why God wanted me around, miserable, useless drunk that I was at the time.

"I dragged myself into an AA meeting that very day. I just kept going and going to meetings because I didn't know what else to do, and I was at my wits' end as to what to do with myself. Couldn't live well, couldn't die well. Being caught in a painful limbo-land in grief and desperation and drowning in shame was like being in my own personal type of hell. Slowly but surely, the fog began to lift. I met one or two people, my world started opening up, and so did I. I spilled my guts from time to time and it felt less like airing my dirty laundry and more like a huge relief. There were people there who had gone through similar things. They understood. Just that alone cut through the blackness for me.

"I have been sober seven full years this month. I can look back into the past, as is my right, given to me by virtue of being clean and sober, and see how powerful my disease was, and how powerful I wasn't. The pitiful picture of me keeled over drunk, with my dead mother in my arms will never leave me. It is that very picture that I need to see in my mind's eye because it keeps me focused on what I have to do to maintain my sanity and my sobriety. There is pain in my past, incredible pain. But my pain makes today possible, and today isn't half bad, to tell you the truth. God wouldn't let me take my own life. He did for me what I could not do for myself. And that was the beginning of a new existence for me."

To review the Eleventh Promise of Sobriety:

~Powerlessness is a key concept in dealing successfully with this disease.

~Spiritual connection is not possible while we are active in our addiction.

~Sometimes we have to perform the action of sitting quietly or praying long before we understand how to pray or what our Higher Power might be.

~The reason that we lose to this disease 100 percent of the time as long as we battle with it is because It uses our own best skills, talents, and thinking to overcome us.

~There is no problem so great nor any human being who has sunk so low as to be exempt from the Eleventh Promise, as long as the willingness and actions follow the desire for relief.

CHAPTER TWELVE
These Promises Will Always Materialize
If We Work for Them

Today I will take a single, positive action that is completely supportive of my sobriety. And today I will take no action to undo the good that I have already done.

Taking strong, positive action is something that is not part of the disease of addiction. Once it is established that actions, not words, are the evidence that one is making positive progress in recovery from drug and alcohol addiction, the gifts begin to materialize. *Trying* to do something is not doing it. Doing something is doing something. Addiction and addictive behavior are about procrastination, empty threats and promises, and broken ultimatums. To get the gifts of sobriety, take the first action.

What is this first action? For some, it is to admit, finally, that despite their embarrassment and sense of defeat, they do, in fact have a problem for which assistance is needed. For others, it is to wait until a firm ultimatum comes from a spouse, friend, or employer and then take action. For a fortunate few, it is to suddenly realize that there is no better time than right now to reach out for help, without giving it any further thought. Often the disease has even overcome one's thought process and it becomes too easy to think our way out of getting help just one more time. Leaping into recovery is the one single action that begins the process of realizing the gifts of sobriety.

The Twelfth Step of Alcoholics Anonymous helps us most in achieving the Twelfth Promise; it states, "Having had a spiritual awakening as the result of these steps, we tried to carry this message to alcoholics, and to practice these principles in all our affairs." When we are ready to take action, whether we are a family member, significant other, co-worker, or the one suffering from the consequences of addiction, there are millions of AA members who are ready to share their experience, strength, and hope with us. Millions of people who work the AA program are ready to work their way through the Twelfth Step when we are ready to join with them to do it. What it takes is someone still suffering from the disease and someone who is well on their way to enjoying the gifts of sobriety. Since the beginning of this program, that is how people have stayed in recovery.

When you are ready to begin working for the gifts of sobriety, you may want to contact your local AA central office. This is a great way to begin working for the gifts. Or, you may already know of someone who has been clean and sober for a significant amount of time. It takes a lot of courage to take the first step, but remember that you are not the first, nor the first hundred thousandth to have done this. The sheer numbers of people living full, complete, healthy lives who once took this same first action have made your way just a bit easier. You will find many who care about your situation. You never have to do this alone.

You and your loved ones deserve and have a birthright to these gifts. Millions of people who are experiencing so much more than mere relief from the disease of addiction have gone ahead of you to prove that it is possible. Reach for what is yours: The gifts of sobriety belong to you if you will believe that they exist and then begin to work for them.

APPENDIX
The Twelve Steps of Alcoholics Anonymous[1]

1. We admitted we were powerless over alcohol—that our lives had become unmanageable.
2. Came to believe that a Power greater than ourselves could restore us to sanity.
3. Made a decision to turn our will and our lives over to the care of God *as we understood Him.*
4. Made a searching and fearless moral inventory of ourselves.
5. Admitted to God, to ourselves, and to another human being the exact nature of our wrongs.
6. Were entirely ready to have God remove all these defects of character.
7. Humbly asked Him to remove our shortcomings.
8. Made a list of all persons we had harmed, and became willing to make amends to them all.
9. Made direct amends to such people wherever possible, except when to do so would injure them or others.
10. Continued to take personal inventory and when we were wrong promptly admitted it.
11. Sought through prayer and meditation to improve our conscious contact with God *as we understood Him,* praying only for knowledge of His will for us and the power to carry that out.
12. Having had a spiritual awakening as the result of these steps, we tried to carry this message to alcoholics, and to practice these principles in all our affairs.

---

1. The Twelve Steps of AA are taken from *Alcoholics Anonymous,* 3d ed., published by AA World Services, Inc., New York, N.Y., 59–60. Reprinted with permission of AA World Services, Inc. (See editor's note on copyright page.)

About the Author

Barbara S. Cole is a licensed psychotherapist and drug and alcohol interventionist, with a private practice in Sherman Oaks and Studio City, California. She has advanced degrees in literature and clinical psychology. She is the author of several books related to self-help and recovery. She worked for many years as a Betty Ford Center counselor and was a director of state licensed and certified drug and alcohol recovery programs. Cole is currently working on two books and completing her doctorate work in psychology.

Hazelden, a national nonprofit organization founded in 1949, helps people reclaim their lives from the disease of addiction. Built on decades of knowledge and experience, Hazelden offers a comprehensive approach to addiction that addresses the full range of patient, family, and professional needs, including treatment and continuing care for youth and adults, research, higher learning, public education and advocacy, and publishing.

A life of recovery is lived "one day at a time." Hazelden publications, both educational and inspirational, support and strengthen lifelong recovery. In 1954, Hazelden published *Twenty-Four Hours a Day*, the first daily meditation book for recovering alcoholics, and Hazelden continues to publish works to inspire and guide individuals in treatment and recovery, and their loved ones. Professionals who work to prevent and treat addiction also turn to Hazelden for evidence-based curricula, informational materials, and videos for use in schools, treatment programs, and correctional programs.

Through published works, Hazelden extends the reach of hope, encouragement, help, and support to individuals, families, and communities affected by addiction and related issues.

For questions about Hazelden publications,
please call **800-328-9000**
or visit us online at **hazelden.org/bookstore.**